NETWORK MARKETING REBOOT

SHIFTS IN CONSUMER BEHAVIOR, HOW TO CHOOSE YOUR BUSINESS & MASTER RESIDUAL INCOME

CHARYLLE WOLFE

CONTENTS

Discover Network Marketing 10 Commandments.
Timeless & ageless wisdom to ensure you have a business of integrity.
Essential and timely information for anyone looking to be successful.

INTRODUCTION

As a smart solopreneur, you are probably looking to spend more time with your family, do the things you genuinely love and enjoy, and earn enough money to sustain you today and in the future. If the network marketing, consumer direct, or direct sales industries are in your chosen path, you are in for a ride, and how bumpy or smooth the journey will be will depend entirely on you.

Without a doubt, consumer behavior has changed over time. A few decades ago, you had to rely on advertisements to learn about products and services, then go to the store if you wanted to give it a try. If the store was closed, you had to wait until the following day. But, today, ordering a product is a click away. You may even have several subscription services running, which would save you time and ensure you don't get disconnected.

Consumers and companies have taken note of this tech-inspired change. The purchasing power is in the hands of the consumer, and companies have to work harder to deliver quality services if they want to continue enjoying market share. Customer service has become a crucial department, since it's at the forefront of building relationships between companies and their clients. A great relationship means satisfied customers and more sales for the company.

The network marketing, direct sales, consumer direct, and MLM industries have not been left behind. Reps are taking full advantage of online platforms such as Facebook, Instagram, Twitter, LinkedIn, and TikTok to build their businesses. Prospecting is done online, meetings are held on Zoom, and podcasts have become a norm in introducing opportunities and sharing wonderful products within the industry.

Through social media alone, representatives can reach their friends through posts and extend this relationship to their friend's circle through sharing and tagging. Videos have also become a sensation. In fact, Facebook videos boast 8 million views a day, according to Sprout Social. You can bet some of these views will have representatives talking about their companies.

That's the power technology has.

However, even with an evolving market, every company still has a single desire at heart; to create sustainability. This is what MLM, network marketing, and direct sales companies offer its representatives. People from all walks of life can create long term and sustainable income for themselves and their families by building businesses. By joining an MLM or network marketing company, you can have the freedom to decide when, how, and where to work. Your income becomes a reflection of your effort, discipline, and skill level.

Granted, these companies don't leave you to work alone. Instead, you would have your teammates for support and training from the company to sharpen your marketing, communication, and network skills. This connection helps you build your income and social circle. By understanding how to build relationships, you are already learning how to build a business in the twenty-first century, where strong emotional connections are a vital part of a customer's purchase journey.

According to the Direct Selling Association (dsa.org), $35.2 billion of goods and services moved through the U.S. economy in 2019 using this business model, from wellness to personal care, and leisure to services.

This book is written to help you understand how the shifts in customer behavior is an advantage for any savvy marketer. By under-standing this, you can take advantage of the market and trends to build your business and create the lifestyle you may be seeking. Will understanding this shift in consumer behavior make work easier for you? Yes. Will your workload be reduced? Probably, but that's not to say you will have a free pass.

Technology is not the only thing that affects customer behavior. Look around and you can almost count the number of trees closeby. The environmental changes also play a massive role in how people buy. The depleted soil and logging are a significant concern for many people, which has led to consumers turning to organic products from companies that care about the environment. The urgency to take better care of the environment has changed consumer behavior so much that the "going green" industry is a trillion-dollars per year. That's how much the environment has changed how people buy.

The rushed life we live today also has a role to play. In a day, you have tons of emails to answer, deadlines to beat, meetings to prepare for and attend, and so on. You also need to spend time with your family and friends and try to sneak in a healthy workout. Life-work imbalance has changed how people buy and influenced how companies sell products and services. More people are willing to work from home as they seek to balance their lives. On the other hand, employers are willing to allow flexible working hours because they realize their employees are more productive when their hours are flexible.

After a long day at work, you look forward to sharing a healthy meal with your family. Research has shown that the food we eat doesn't have enough nutrients to nourish our bodies; thus, we have to rely on supplements to bridge this nutritional gap and keep our bodies healthy and strong. We have to adopt long-term, healthier habits, such as working out, maintaining a healthy weight, and meditating and other mind quieting activities to stay well. Granted, all these health dynamics change what we pick up from the store.

Anyone who has been in the MLM, consumer direct, network marketing, and direct sales industries will tell you that choosing a company that you will be genuinely excited about is not easy. There are many things to consider, such as a company's culture, compensation plan, and so on. If you are not careful, you may end up frustrated and/or broke.

It's tempting to think that MLM, direct sales, and network marketing are avenues that can make quick money. However, the truth is that you have to be willing to work hard and share the opportunity with others if you want to see results. Anyone can join the industry, and with the right skills, anyone can succeed. If you are interested in building a sustainable business through ethical, proven, marketing concepts, and understanding how consumer behavior impacts your business, pour a cup of coffee, tea, or other beverage of choice and join me.

CHAPTER ONE: IN THE BEGINNING... MY STORY

"When I stand before God at the end of my life, I would hope that I would not have a single bit of talent left, and could say, "I used everything you gave me."

— *ERMA BOMBECK*

I DEDICATE THIS CHAPTER TO FRIENDS AND READERS WHO WERE kind enough to give me constructive criticism and encouragement to add my own story to this book. So, thank you all for your input and helping me make it better.

There I was—a new mom with a new baby, driving to my first day of work after Maternity Leave. Sigh… Don't get me wrong. I wanted to go back to work. After all, I had a degree and coveted job for my area; it was a job that others my age and with the same education would die for. So, what was the problem then? I couldn't really put my finger on it. I wanted to go back to work and pick up where I left off, but I also wanted to stay home. It was hard, and I felt an incredible amount of guilt (I do have to pause here and mention that I had an incredibly supportive family who cared for our son during the day. A few years later, we had another child, and I know both of our sons were extremely cared for and loved, and for that, I'm extremely grateful).

So it began—my ride on the proverbial hamster wheel. Getting up early, getting everybody ready, dropping them off, getting to work, picking everyone up, coming home late, making dinner, bathing/play time, having way too little sleep... Wash, rinse, repeat. I really was contemplating whether it was all worth it, but I decided to chalk it up to hormones and just needing to readjust after having been gone on maternity leave. Besides, isn't this what everyone else was doing? Isn't this how you "make it?" No pain, no gain, right?

Many people ask me, "What made you decide to stay home?" The answer is that it was more of an evolution melded together with flashes of clarity. It felt more like a tug of war between my mind, emotions, and societal expectations. My decision to become a stay-at-home mom is in no way meant to judge or criticize any parent who is trying their utmost to juggle a career and family life. Anyone who sets out on the adventure of parenthood and a career, in whatever setting that happens to be in, has my utmost admiration and respect. Our decision was the right one for our family. The moment I can point to that started it all for us was when I received a direct mail piece that was so compelling that I couldn't throw it away or get it off my mind. I couldn't tell what the product was, or if there was a product, but the stories were so captivating, I decided to call the number on the inside.

The company turned out to be a network marketing company and leader in the weight loss industry, and the mail piece was a prospecting—or recruiting—tool. This was my first exposure to this type of business model, but since I was looking to shed the weight I had gained during pregnancy, I was willing to give it a shot. The products turned out to be incredible. Within five weeks, I had lost all but a couple of pounds and was wearing my normal clothes again. Yes, I was ecstatic and started thinking I could be successful as a distributor, so I bought in at the highest level I could in order to maximize my commission. I'm not sure what my husband truly thought when all the boxes with product inventory appeared at our home, but he was supportive.

I got right to work learning everything I could, calling my sponsor frequently, becoming a product of the product and doing everything they said to acquire customers and get rid of that inventory. I told myself that it should be easy. After all, I had a powerful product testimony of my own, so you'd have to be out of your mind not to want these products—right? At the time, between 55-60% of the American population was overweight, so these products should "fly" off my shelf. I was coachable and did everything my upline told me to do, and I did get some customers, but it wasn't as easy as I'd heard it was on training calls. Not to mention, I had to buy a certain amount of product from the company each month to qualify for commissions from those in my downline. It was stressful, but I didn't know any better, so we just buckled down and went for it. There was no choice; we were all in.

Soon, I started using the same direct mail piece I had received so I could grow a team of my own faster. Things were working; my team started to move and grow, and we started experiencing some success.

Weeks turned into months, then a couple of years as I continued to work at my outside job until we added another boy to our family, and the timing seemed to be right for me to become a stay-at-home mom. All seemed to be going according to plan.

At this point, the Internet was still in its early stages, as far as e-commerce went, and the field was wide open. I built a website to sell my company products online and did quite well. *Whew!* My struggle to get customers in the beginning was finally behind me. I had hit on something that worked, and worked well.

I was also able to recruit and sponsor others into the company using the internet, and I ended up with teams in several different countries. One of the high points of my time with that company was when I travelled to Australia in order to meet the wonderful people on my team and take part in a training for them. It was quite humbling, standing at the front of the room and looking out at the audience, knowing I was earning income every month, not only from my efforts, but from almost everyone in that room who fell within my pay line. It was the first training of that kind I had ever done, and it probably wasn't very good, but it will remain one of the highest points and most cherished memories of that season in my life.

We were now international, enjoying a six-figure income, and so blessed. It was a real kick to get my income report each month, look through it, and see how currencies were converted into dollars. It was also amazing seeing all the names from different countries. I felt like I had *arrived!*

All seemed to be in place, and we were rocking along healthily and happily. We built another house, took some great vacations, and I was home with our kids. Mission accomplished.

You've all heard about hindsight being 20/20. I used to think life was backwards—we should have foresight, so we could see into the future to make better decisions and avoid life's pitfalls. I still think that sometimes, but that's the way it is. God doesn't consult with me on these things, no matter how awesome that would be. Can I get an AMEN here?

Within a few years of that incredible trip, some unfortunate events at that company occurred, and it became apparent that I had hit the pinnacle—the ceiling, the brick wall. Some cracks started to appear that I couldn't quite put my finger on. The direct mail piece no longer worked, several changes in company leadership made it feel like we were a ship without a sail, and most discouraging of all was that the people I had recruited into the business were no longer able to achieve the same milestones that I had. Things seemed to be coming apart at the seams and everything was going drastically wrong.

It was a painful decision to make, but I knew the right thing to do was to leave that company. This is the part where most of you are probably thinking that I'm nuts. Who would walk away from a six-figure income? Certainly not a sane individual. But… sometimes, things are just the right thing to do, no matter how much income it is.

Now what do I do? I was in love with the home business concept. I knew I couldn't or wouldn't go back to working for someone else. The sheer thought of returning to the rat race and office politics and living life at warp speed made my skin crawl. I also knew that wherever I went next had to be different in a few key areas.

Since I had self-assigned myself the task of finding a new company home, not only for myself, but for anyone in my team who still trusted me enough to go with me, there were several requirements on my list. First, there needed to be a low barrier to entrepreneurship. I wasn't interested in investing thousands of dollars. Second, I didn't want to have to purchase and stock inventory, ship orders, collect money, or deliver anything. I also wanted a product line that would appeal to the masses, rather than niche specific or trendy products that someone would only buy for a short season in their life. The price point was also important—if most people could afford them comfortably, and the products were good, it would be a fit.

I won't sugarcoat anything here; it was scary. There was no way to know for certain if I could duplicate past success—here's where that "being able to see into the future" superpower would've been helpful. Finding a new company home was not taken lightly. It took a little time and some research, but we landed safely and have been with the same company over 15 years. Not only has it been a long-term home for us, but many of those who came with us are still here too and *thriving!*

This business model has definitely come of age. I've found it to be one of the fairest and most level-playing fields around. People from all walks of life and backgrounds are crafting a better lifestyle for themselves and their families. It truly has been the answer to a lot of people's prayers. You can choose to be your own boss, work from anywhere, experience more work/life balance, and still afford a lifestyle that suits your goals.

One of the reasons I chose to write this book was to give some insight into how consumer behavior has shifted over the last few years and package it in a way that is easy to follow and makes sense to the average reader. How anybody who chooses this business model for themselves can dramatically increase their chances of success by understanding the marketplace landscape and what consumers are looking for.

Insight into the marketplace is only one third of the equation, however; you have to consider the company itself and you. That is why I created the worksheets at the end that will help you not only navigate how to evaluate a company, but so you can also have a thoughtful self-analysis in order to assess yourself as well. If you follow through with this exercise, you will be more informed and educated, which can help you find the right fit and make the best decision for your future.

This endeavor has been a labor of love, and I wish you the very best! Your dreams are waiting for you, so *get busy!*

CHAPTER TWO: RELIANCE ON TECH

*"We often hear people talk about the concept of
'uberization,' where a new technology completely turns
an industry on its head and forces us to rethink the
way things have always been done. No industry will
remain untouched by these forces."*

— *KLAUS SCHWAB*

IN AUGUST 1989, PEOPLE WOULD HAVE THOUGHT THAT ANOTHER "normal" year was coming to an end. The World Wide Web went live, but there was no fanfare, global press, and fireworks. People around the world didn't know about the internet, and even if they did, the usage was still like a drop in the ocean.

Fast forward to today—where the internet is not only in most homes around the globe, but it is also the new normal way of doing business. Every company is fighting to get a piece of the pie, including the direct sales industry. In addition, with the constant change in technology use, it's only natural to assume that things are not business as usual.

The use of digital technologies has contributed immensely to changes in consumer behavior and how purchase decisions are made. Through social media, consumers can share, contribute, and access information at their fingertips.

A few years back, the nature of doing business was different from what we know today. Stores were opened at a certain time, operated for X hours, and closed down by about 7 PM. If you didn't make it to the store during working hours, you had to wait until the next day, never mind if you needed something urgently. Today, these same stores run for 24 hours a day to cater to the 24-hour economy. People hold more than one job and work longer hours than they did a few decades ago.

The demand for the convenience of having your goods delivered to your doorstep has also seen the rise of online shops that are now willing to go that extra mile for their client. Think about this—when you want to buy something, what's the first thing you do? If you are like most people, you would probably search for information about that specific item on the internet, read a few reviews, and check whether the purchase is worth it. If you need more information, you would ask a friend, family member, or post a question on forums like Reddit, Quora, and Facebook groups.

This change has greatly influenced how businesses operate, the level of unemployment, and how consumers buy. However, before we get to that and why network marketing may be a good fit for you, let's first consider how technology has changed how we do business today.

Social Media and a New Way of Doing Business

I'm sure you have heard the phrase "numbers don't lie." According to various statistics, social media continues to be the most popular online activity. It's so popular that researchers have found that 22% of the time spent online is spent on a social media platform such as Facebook, Instagram, Twitter, and Pinterest. Let's take a closer look at these numbers.

Research by Statista, a business data platform, shows that at least

78.2% of the US population was connected to the internet in 2010. In 2018, this number had shot up to 275 million internet users. Social media alone accounted for 79% of the online population in 2019, which was a 2% increase from 2018. This would mean there were approximately 247 million people on social media alone. The platform suggests that 317.1 million people will be connected to the internet by 2023, which will see the rise in social media use. Insane, right?

This overwhelming evidence has made businesses develop a strong online presence, with social media being the main focus because of the traffic it drives to a site. There is no denying that social media has changed the business world and consumer behavior.

For instance, people born between 1978 and 1994 were the first people to use the internet. Naturally, they expected to get information at their fingertips and to have the freedom to control the information they consumed. As a result, they stopped trusting traditional marketing tools such as TV and radio, and even frowned upon the use of cold calls.

Naturally, this led businesses to change how they did business and adapt their marketing strategies to meet consumer needs, meeting on social media platforms instead of bombarding them on TV. This was also when people trusted Yahoo (Bing) and were only experimenting with Google.

With the launch of Myspace in 2003, Facebook in 2004, and Twitter in 2006, things took a different turn. More people started spending time online, and when Instagram came by in 2010 and Snapchat in 2011, things simply exploded. By then, the baby boomer generation was already online, and companies recognized the need to reach this "social media generation" if they wanted to push their products and services.

HOW SOCIAL MEDIA HAS CHANGED HOW BUSINESSES OPERATE

1. Through targeted marketing

In just a decade, social media has left an undeniable mark on the business world. You see, marketing and advertising are the most influential aspects of social media; this is because it has made it possible to put your products and services in front of the exact consumer you want to target.

Let's think about this for a moment.

You are seated in your dentist's office waiting for your appointment when you notice a magazine article on forex trading. Out of curiosity, you pop the page open, but you are called in before you gather "enough" information.

Once your appointment is over, you do what anybody else would have done: look for the information online. After reading a few articles to satisfy your curiosity, you then head to Facebook to catch up on what people are doing, only to be bombarded by a couple Forex trading ads. A few days or a week later, these ads disappear into thin air.

Or, perhaps you've been thinking about refinancing your mortgage, so you've been researching. Suddenly, your social media is flooded with ads about loans and refinancing a mortgage.

Using the information gathered by search engines and social media platforms, companies target customers based on their interests and what they search for online. Before social media, businesses had to seek out websites and buy ad space, but now, all they rely on are the metrics provided by social media sites to reach you.

2. Consumers are in control

In the traditional business model, consumers had to call the company if they had a question or complaint. After the introduction of the World Wide Web, emails became the new form of communication between consumers and companies, but even that had its drawbacks. For starters, companies could choose not to respond to complaints, and there was nothing consumers could do about that.

Social media has leveled the field, creating visibility for everyone. Companies are more in touch with their clients and able to answer questions in real time, which has increased customer satisfaction. In a way, this has taken power away from the businesses and given it back to the consumers. If you are an angry customer, you can voice your opinion for millions of users to see, putting the company on the spot. This transparency has forced businesses to invest in customer service, which is a good thing.

3. The rise of organic advertising

Online advertising is nothing new, but past models like PPC ads, seemed forced due to their in-your-face stigma. Banner ads were no better, and pop-ups were frowned upon. Likewise, sponsored ads seemed "fake," and people hardly paid attention to them.

With the rise of social media marketing, ads are now more organic, and they don't seem to interfere with how someone uses them. For instance, you can scroll through your Facebook or Instagram feed and pass a few ads on your timeline that don't actually scream advertisements. This non-interference makes them seem natural, and because they don't bother anyone, people don't really mind them.

Also, companies can interact with their audience and promote valuable content without appearing pushy and needy. This leads to brand growth and free marketing through word of mouth, sharing links, and tagging friends on the things that customers find exciting and valuable.

Another advantage is the availability to disseminate information through different forms, such as images, videos, text, and infographics. Because businesses are not restrained to formalities on social platforms, they can package their content easily and either formally or informally. Companies can also mix the latter two, depending on the occasion and communication being pushed out. This includes the use of memes, emojis, jokes, and even slang.

4. Leveled the competition field

Before the internet, businesses needed to have tens of thousands of dollars to advertise on mainstream media. Think of radio, TV, and newspapers—even today, these three are some of the costliest forms of advertising available. The disadvantage with newspapers, for instance, is that nobody buys them anymore. TVs aren't any better because people either change the channel when commercials come on or find an excuse to rush to the washroom, pour another cup of coffee, or grab a beer from the fridge. When an ad comes on the radio, most people switch to a different station.

Besides those disadvantages, small businesses and startups could not compete fairly with multi-million-dollar companies. Consider that local bakery whose bagels are to die for; even though they have a great product, they probably don't have the financial coffer to pay for ads that will run for weeks—sometimes months—on TV and radio.

However, with a fraction of that budget, they can learn and leverage the digital space to reach customers. Surprisingly, social media has a wider reach than traditional media, which makes it even more valuable.

Technology Has Changed How People Earn Money

When we were young, our parents told us to study hard, go to college, and secure a steady job, the latter specifically with good benefits being the best option. If we didn't, our lives would be filled with nightmares as we scraped through life, wondering what the future held.

This fear made us work hard, get good grades, and go to college. However, it was time to look for a job, a different reality struck—suddenly, everyone had a college degree to show the unimpressed human resource manager. Quickly, we realized that we had to do something different, offer something different if we wanted to secure a remotely decent job.

Fast forward to when companies started advertising online. Blogging became a respectable income stream and Tik Tok and Instagram influencers started earning more than a regular office manager. That's the power that digital marketing has had on the job market.

Tech skills are in demand as people, companies, and organizations crave websites and content. Consumers, on the other hand, are fishing around for the most valuable information and the company that offers what they need. If these two needs were to be merged, the company would make a killing by selling its products and services, and the consumer would receive what they needed. Then, the tech expert would also earn money by either linking the company with the consumer through ads or by facilitating what the company needed to reach the consumer through content.

This is kind of a win-win situation.

What's interesting, however, is that none of these people needed to be located in a physical store to make things happen. For instance, the company could have a virtual office, the tech expert could be working in their garage in pajamas, and the consumer could have been miles away and binge-watching Netflix while they made their order.

Heck, even Netflix became a revolution from buying DVDs and visiting movie theatres when their popularity spread by the internet and recognized convenience of watching movies at home. Sites like Amazon, Spotify, Ebay, and others have become a steady income stream for thousands of people. One doesn't have to look too far— maybe even past their own mirror—to know someone who has morphed one of these opportunities into a profitable side hustle, or even career level income. They would rather travel the world and blog about it while making a six-figure income along the way, hence the coinage of the term "digital nomads." Social Media Influencers have also revolutionized advertising. An influencer with a large following and high engagement rate can leverage this from companies by offering to promote their products and services.

Think of it this way—the company needs to get its products and services in front of their target market. The influencer has thousands of people following them on Instagram that fall within the company's market niche. Naturally, the company would want to approach the influencer and ask for a "shout out," so they can put their products or services on their timeline for a fee. This is by far more affordable for the company than it would be to schedule a TV ad for a few minutes a day.

The unemployment rate has increased with the recent COVID-19 pandemic, as companies and small businesses struggle to remain afloat. According to research by Fact Tank, the number of unemployed Americans has risen by more than 14 million between February and May 2020. Companies have also adopted working remotely to ensure their operations are not affected. The technology advancement we have has dramatically helped keep companies afloat and money in people's pockets.

Even those who have lost their jobs have dived into working remotely by selling their skills online. The number of freelancers has increased, as has the number of courses offered online. Experts at Just Answer say that freelancer income payout increased in April, which was 23% higher than previous months.

The number of experts on the platform saw the most prolific experts earn as much as $60,000 in a month. This includes lawyers, antique appraisers, and auto mechanics. Flex Jobs—another platform —reported that demand for experts increased by more than 24% from March to April. So, even though the pandemic has increased unemployment rate and affected millions of people drastically, remote work has seen a surge in both jobs and experts for task handling.

This is all how technology and its numerous opportunities have made earning—even in tough times—readily available.

TECHNOLOGY HAS BROUGHT A SHIFT IN CONSUMER BEHAVIOR

Using the traditional marketing model, consumers have followed a funnel when buying a product. The top was full of people who were just becoming aware of the product and brand; then, they eventually went through a few steps until they finally purchased the product. Customers" drop off" at each level, with only a handful making it to the final stage: purchase.

Although this process is still followed today, it's safe to say that it's no longer as linear a process as it used to be. Customers can now hop between stages of the funnel in multiple companies thanks to the internet. Buyers can move from curious prospect to purchase within minutes, or from trigger to consideration, then purchase.

However, even with this, we have to agree that customers still follow three main steps: first, the trigger, then the "ok I'm interested to know more," and then, finally, the buy button.

- **The trigger**—During this stage, consumers realize they need a particular product or service.
- **The first moment of truth**—Here, the customer researches and gathers information about the product. It can also be called the research stage. Today, it has become the most crucial part in the purchasing process.
- **The second moment of truth**—Once you buy and use the product, you would then decide if you liked the product or not, now that you have experienced it. If you like the product and the service the company accorded you, you could become a loyal customer. If not, you may decide to keep looking.

Traditionally, you would have transitioned through these stages with the help of a sales representative—but today, the journey starts with search engines. You would now jump from one site to another; click here and there until you arrive at the answer you are searching for.

Granted, most of the searches online are from mobile phones, with Google reporting that 75% searches are credited to mobile devices as of 2019. Out of these searches, 65% will suggest shopping through mobile phones at least once a month.

This information suggests that you would enter a store (online or a brick and mortar store) with the first two purchase stages complete; you didn't need a salesperson.

Throughout the process, your behavior would be influenced by certain factors. These include:

- **Personal factors, such as your interests and opinions**. These are often affected by demographics, age, culture, background, profession, and gender.
- **Psychological factors that look at your perception and attitudes, and how they influence your response to a**

particular marketing campaign. Your ability to comprehend information, how you perceive your needs, and your attitude will play a part in your buying decision.

- **Social factors, such as peers, family, friends, and social media**. Under this category, your income, education level, and social class will also play a role.

All this information is great, but how does it help us understand how consumer behavior has changed? Let's look at one of the most popular factors: social factors.

Human beings are social. We always prefer to belong in a community of people and to have a "click" with those we most identify with, either as family or friends. Once we find this group, we imitate them in a bid to be socially accepted in that society.

These groups—for instance, your family—play a significant role in how you make purchases. There are preferences you developed since you were a child by watching how your parents, sisters, brothers, and uncles prefer certain products over others. Some of the products you buy may be a result of something you hated or loved when you were a kid.

The role you play in society will also influence your buying behavior; if you are in a high-income bracket, your buying behavior will be influenced by your position. You may, for instance, splurge more on luxury items or prefer certain brands because of your economic status. That would be the same way a staff member will buy a different brand from the chief executive officer, even though they work in the same company.

That's why you will see your friend on Instagram doing something, and you will automatically want to do the same. If all your friends have good jobs and you don't, you may start to feel segregated and left out when they discuss how work was or how Linda from finance made a nasty comment about Stacy.

This information will land on every social media platform you are in. For instance, you may join a job board on Facebook and comment on some of the jobs you are interested in. After that, perhaps you join LinkedIn and apply for a few jobs before doing the same on Twitter by following links to certain jobs. A few moments later, you might look toward Google for jobs you are interested in and apply to several posts there.

Do this for a while, and your Facebook feed will have suggestions of job boards you can join, probably with the same job interests you applied for. LinkedIn will also send you notifications of jobs you may be interested in, and you may even see some ads from the companies you Googled.

All these started from seeing and hearing your friends talk about their jobs, which elicited feelings of want and inadequacy and a need to fit in. This is consumer behavior in action. Let's look at another example for the sake of emphasis.

You log in to your Instagram and see a beautiful shoe, so you like it. As you scroll through, ads start appearing of the same kind of shoe or something similar. You double-tap on a few more, and now you can't stop seeing shoes on your timeline. As annoying as it is, you told Instagram bots that you really loved shoes, and, naturally, they showed you more of what you loved.

So, even though you don't talk to a salesman, your purchase will still be influenced by other people's opinions. But where is the sales rep you used to rely on for information?

Today, a sales rep is seen as a trusted advisor and have become thought leaders in their fields. These are the people you would turn to when you can't find answers on your own. These are also the people who write sales copy and lead magnets for companies.

That's why businesses have realized that power is in the hands of the buyer. With the internet at their fingertips, buyers can conduct in-depth research that is replacing the need for companies to pitch products and services. Instead, it's become more beneficial to build trust with consumers and provide them with useful and relevant information that's easily accessible through whatever device they decide to use.

CHAPTER SUMMARY

In this chapter, we have learned that:

- Social media platforms have introduced a new way to conduct business.
- Technology has opened up new avenues of earning money.
- Technology has brought a shift in consumer behavior by giving power back to the consumer.

In the next chapter, we will talk about healthy lifestyles and choices, and how they have affected the market.

CHAPTER THREE: HEALTHY LIFESTYLE. CHOICE, CONDUCT, AND PREVENTION

Multi-level marketing, network marketing, and direct sales are the names used by those in that type of company to describe how their business models work. Their detractors call what they do, 'One of those pyramid schemes,' with a snarl. These companies are not pyramid schemes. They are a legitimate way for some people to make some side money, and sometimes to literally build their own businesses.

— *DAVE RAMSEY*

It's New Year's Eve. Weighing in at 300 plus pounds, you promise yourself, for the third year in a row, to do something about it. You sit and reminisce of what you will do, research the different weight-loss strategies, and finally settle on something you think is manageable.

However, weight is not the only issue. Since you are almost immobile, thanks to the weight, you vow that another year won't end when you don't have a job. Something has to give, and that degree you spent four years studying will have to start giving you some returns. You pick your laptop and spruce up your resume, then apply for a couple of entry-level jobs and shop online for comfortable shoes and workout clothes.

Two months down the line, you have added weight, haven't been called for an interview, and feel worse than you did at the beginning of the year.

This scenario is a story shared by many people around the world. A study by Statista suggests that the top resolutions for most Americans are making healthier choices, both in their eating habits and finances. For finances, most people look to spend wisely and save more, whereas health is mostly associated with having a more active lifestyle and weight loss.

Other resolutions include improving mental health and practicing meditation and mindfulness. Getting more sleep, learning a new skill, and traveling were also on the top of the list. But why is health and money at the top of a majority of (51%) lists?

It's not a surprise why most people want to lose weight when 42.4% of the population is obese. This is according to the CDC. Young adults, between ages 20 and 39, are the most affected. Although they make up the most active and productive population, they account for 40% of obese people in America. 44.8% of middle-aged adults are also obese.

There are numerous benefits to maintaining a healthy weight. Still, most people fail to see it through because they lack the motivation and drive needed to maintain a consistent weight loss journey. Out of those who make it, some won't have the required drive to keep the weight off, and within a few months of losing it, they are back to where they started.

For most people, losing weight is associated with many things. For example, being overweight increases the likelihood of lifestyle diseases like heart disease, diabetes, and high blood pressure. Also, some forms of cancer, such as breast cancer, are said to be exacerbated by a high BMI (Body Mass Index). Sleep apnea is also a result of the same.

Someone who is already at the risk of getting one of these illnesses may be motivated to lose weight, which, according to statistics, is around 73% of people.. For such people, weight loss is a ticket to living a longer and higher quality of life. With this, they can experience the wonderful things life has to offer.

Social shame is also another reason why people want to lose weight. When you are overweight, social shaming becomes part of your day as people give you those weird glances, and even comment on how you look. This can lead to body insecurities, self-esteem, and confidence issues. These cause anxiety and depression. When people lose weight, however, they feel good about themselves, improve their self-confidence and esteem, and even become proactive in other areas of their lives, especially their social life.

Speaking of energy, many people with a high BMI also feel that they lack the energy to do simple things like walk around the block, play with their kids for a long period, or finish house chores. That's why 49% of Americans who want to lose weight say that they need an energy boost to do the simple things in life.

However, heart disease, diabetes, and high blood pressure are not the only reasons why people want to lose weight—statistics suggest that 19% of overweight people want to lose weight because they experience painful joints. As you can imagine, being overweight puts pressure on your joints, especially your knees, leading to wear and tear, which then promotes the onset of arthritis. Because of the pain, immobility increases, which only worsens weight gain.

No wonder the dietary supplements market is so successful. In 2019, it was estimated to be $123.28 billion USD and projected to expand with an 8.2% growth rate a year. Health concerns, changing lifestyles, and dietary issues are the main driving factors. Also, people have developed an astounding interest in sports and nutrition that focus on physical strength.

The rapid urbanization and increase in disposable income, coupled with the awareness of health issues, are the main factors expected to propel the industry in the coming period. Dietary supplements lead to healthier lifestyles because they provide the necessary nutrition for a healthy body, which has also contributed to the growth of the industry.

Technology has also played a role, mainly as a selling medium for manufacturers. Tech provides access to information where buyers can learn more about products from the comfort of their homes. People check reviews, read about the manufacturer's policies, research ingredients, and consult with experts before deciding if the product is worth trying.

Tech has also taken things a little further, especially where e-commerce is concerned. With a credit card, you can now order your supplements online and have them delivered to your doorstep within a few weeks, days, and sometimes even hours. This convenience encourages consumers to order and use products that they would have otherwise been too lazy to rush to the store for. Before we dive into this, let's take a look at the top five health issues in America, and how what you eat can affect your health.

TOP 5 HEALTH ISSUES IN AMERICA

1. Heart Disease

When you think about it, the heart is a small but amazing organ. It pumps oxygen and nutrients throughout the body, beating at least 100,000 times and pushing around 2,000 gallons of blood within a single day. Besides pumping oxygen and nutrients to the rest of the body, the heart is also responsible for taking the waste products away from body tissues, sustaining life, and promoting health. That's why getting heart disease can be deadly for anyone.

By definition, heart disease is any condition that affects your heart's structure and how your heart functions. For instance, abnormal rhythms, coronary heart disease, congestive heart failure, heart attack, stroke, rheumatic heart disease, vascular disease would all fall under this category, and these examples are some of the most common illnesses associated with the heart.

These diseases are also the leading cause of death among men and women in America and worldwide, though it is more prevalent in men than in women. According to various medical practitioners, most heart diseases result from plaque building up in the walls of the arteries. As the buildup starts, the arteries narrow and make it difficult for blood to flow around the body. This increases the chances of a heart attack and stroke, and it can also give rise to other illnesses such as angina, heart failure, and arrhythmias.

What's interesting, however, is that heart disease can be controlled, and you can do a lot to lower your chances. For instance, if you smoke, you are two times likely to get a heart illness. On the other hand, quitting would reduce your chances. Your cholesterol levels would also increase your risk if you have a total level of 200: HDL (good) cholesterol levels lower than 40, triglycerides over 150, and LDL (bad cholesterol) levels over 160.

Your cholesterol levels are not the only determining factor, but doctors admit that it plays a significant role. Another factor includes high blood pressure. Research has shown that more than 50 million people battle hypertension, which is one of the reasons why heart disease is so common. You can reduce your chances of getting high blood pressure by maintaining a healthy diet, reducing your salt intake, and working out the required amount each day.

Stress and anger are also leading causes of heart illnesses. In the world we live in, stress is a normal part of our everyday lives, but when we fail to control it, our anxiety and anger flare up, which can cause problems, especially if this scenario happens often. Managing your stress levels and anger flares is, thus, one way to control getting heart disease.

2. Cancer

This is the one thing that causes thin, nervous sweat to flow down everyone's spine when they visit a doctor. When you are healthy, your cells usually divide and replace themselves naturally. With cancer, your cells would divide uncontrollably. A tumor is basically a cluster of such abnormal cells, but not all tumors are cancerous. The difference is that malignant tumors spread to other body tissues, crowding them and drawing nutrients that the healthy cells need.

Like heart disease, cancer is also considered a lifestyle illness, which means that it's possible to prevent it. Research shows that with the knowledge we have today, we can prevent about 50% of cancer cases and around 50% of cancer deaths.

As a preventive measure, you would need to avoid tobacco, including secondary smoke from others who partake instead. Eating a healthy diet and especially reducing your intake of saturated fats and red meat can also help. Instead, increase your intake of fruits, whole grains, and vegetables. As usual, you can't escape from a daily dose of exercise, so include that in your day. Working out will also help you stay lean, which is another way to reduce your risk of getting cancer.

Although drinking is not entirely shunned, you will need to limit yourself to a drink a day. Of course, it's always better if you can do away with it altogether. You also need to reduce exposure to radiation and industrial and environmental toxins and avoid infections that contribute to cancer, such as HIV, human papillomavirus, and hepatitis. You should also be getting a good night's sleep and enough vitamin D.

3. Diabetes

Diabetes is responsible for 3% of deaths in America, though what's surprising is that one in every four people don't actually know that they have diabetes. This would account for approximately seven million people. Diabetes refers to several illnesses that involve problems with the hormone insulin. In a healthy body, the pancreas releases insulin whose primary use is to help the body store and use sugar. It's also used to store fat received from the food we eat.

When you have diabetes, your body releases very little to no insulin. Your body could also have a difficult time responding appropriately to insulin. This causes blood glucose/sugar levels to be too high. When you have Type 1 diabetes, your body is unable to make enough insulin; on the other hand, Type 2 means your body is unable to use insulin well. In both instances, your blood sugar becomes higher than it should, which may cause serious problems.

For instance, high sugar levels can damage your eyes, nerves, and kidneys. It can also lead to heart disease, stroke, and in some cases, the need to have a limb amputated. For pregnant women, gestational diabetes is common, especially in women with a high BMI. A simple blood test can help determine if you have diabetes.

It's important to note that Type 1 diabetes usually appears when you are young or during adolescence. In fact, Type 1 diabetes is said to be caused by genetics and some viruses, although the exact cause is largely unknown. Scientists think that the body's immune system mistakenly destroys the insulin-producing cells, resulting in low insulin production. Type 1 diabetes is thus not a result of the lifestyle decisions you make. When we speak of diabetes in this chapter, we will be referring to Type 2 diabetes, which is a result of poor health choices.

Type 2 diabetes used to be referred to as adult-diabetes, but today, more children are getting it as the level of child obesity continues to rise. Like Type 1 diabetes, there is no cure for Type 2 diabetes, but making different lifestyle changes can help manage the disease significantly.

Usually, symptoms can range from severe to mild. Hunger and fatigue is usually the first sign. The food you eat is converted into insulin, which your cells use for energy; however your cells are unable to take glucose without insulin. Thus, when your cells cannot take enough glucose, or it resists the insulin your body produces, they would signal your body to get more food, making you hungrier than usual.

Also, you may need to eliminate more often and feel thirstier. On average, you should use the restroom around seven times within 24 hours. Your mouth is also likely to be dry and your skin itchy, coupled with blurred vision. Other symptoms include yeast infections, numb and painful feet, soreness, and cuts that won't heal. This is especially true in Type 2 diabetes.

However, since diabetes is mainly a lifestyle disease, you can prevent it through simple shifts in everyday activities. Your diet, for instance, is the first thing you should watch. Plenty of fiber may help you reduce risks by improving your blood sugar level, lowering the risk of heart disease, and promoting weight loss. The foods you need include beans, nuts, fruits, and vegetables.

According to The National Library of Medicine, whole grain bread is far better than white bread. Whole grain bread contains higher levels of fiber and protein, which are essential in slowing down the absorption of sugar in your bloodstream. This keeps your blood sugar levels steady and reduces your risk of diabetes. Obesity is also a culprit here, like in any other lifestyle disease. Every pound you lose will improve your health. The results can be so dramatic that a study found that a reduction of 7% of your initial body weight reduced the risk of diabetes in participants by almost 60%!

Instead of opting for fad diets whose results are not sustainable or with no well-known effects, it would be in your best interest to maintain an active lifestyle. You may not know it, but weight loss increases your cell's sensitivity to insulin, which means that you only need a little insulin to keep your blood sugar in check.

A study in people with pre-diabetes found that moderate and low-impact workouts increased insulin sensitivity by 51%, whereas high-intensity workouts increased the participants' sensitivity by 85%. Although this effect occurred on workout days only, the result can be tremendous if you even just commit to low impact workouts, such as walking. The best exercises, however, are aerobics, strength training, and interval training (High Intensity Interval Training, or HIIT).

You should also make water your primary beverage because it will help you avoid drinks that are high in sugar, such as soda and punch. Quit smoking, watch your food portion sizes, avoid sedentary behavior, and get enough vitamin D.

4. Kidney Disease

In 2017 alone, at least 50,000 people died of kidney disease. This accounts for 1.8% of the total deaths in America. Like the heart, kidneys play a vital role in keeping our bodies healthy. In most cases, our kidneys only just begin to receive the appreciation they deserve when they start failing. However, when they are busy removing waste and extra fluid from your body, you hardly notice them. In a single day, the kidney will filter at least 200 quarts of blood and make about one to two quart of urine.

Urine and excess water may be what the kidney is known for, but their work is far more than that. For starters, kidneys control blood pressure. Kidneys rely on pressure to work, and thus control it by taking charge of fluid levels. Red blood cell production is also highly dependent on your kidneys. The hormone erythropoietin tells the bone marrow to make more red cells when it's required. The kidney produces this hormone, which means that your kidneys are responsible for the energy you need in a day.

Your bones are also highly dependent on your kidneys' health. That's because you need your kidneys to absorb calcium and phosphorus, which are the minerals that make your bones strong. Your kidneys balance the amount of calcium and phosphorus required for the body, so you can have just the right amount. Kidneys also balance your body's pH levels, lowering and increasing acid in your body as needed.

So, when your kidneys start to fail, all these bodily functions will suffer. To prevent kidney disease, aim for a healthy weight, get enough sleep, and—for the umpteenth time—stop smoking. Also, limit your drinking, since too much alcohol can add extra calories and increase your blood pressure. Naturally, this would end up giving your kidneys more work than necessary, leading to weight gain. If you plan to consume alcohol, women should limit drinking to one drink a day, whereas men should limit their intake to two drinks.

Healthy meals are also of great benefit. In particular, choose foods that are great for your kidneys, such as veggies, fruits, and whole grains. Obviously, make physical activity like jogging and aerobics part of your daily routine. Explore ways to reduce stress and cope with problems because doing so will improve your emotional and physical health. Do your best to manage diabetes, high blood pressure, and heart disease.

5. Mental Health

Mental health concerns may be on the rise as people learn more about it. According to The National Insititute of Mental Health, suicide killed close to 50,000 people in 2017. The majority of these cases are believed to have stemmed from mental health issues. Each year, many more are affected by mental illness, such as in 2018 when

19.1% of adults in the country—or 47.6 million people—battled mental illness. In other words, that would be one in every five adults. 16.5% of youths, seventeen years or less, also suffered from mental health issues.

The most common mental health illnesses are anxiety, depression, bipolar disorder, and schizophrenia. These conditions affect a person's mood, feelings, and behavior, directly impacting how a person feels, thinks, and acts. Note that mental illness and poor mental health are different; a person can have poor mental health and not be diagnosed with a mental illness.

Mental health increases the risk for many types of physical health issues, such as stroke, heart disease, and Type 2 diabetes. However, the opposite is also true—if you suffer from a chronic illness, you are also susceptible to mental health illness. Common signs of mental illness include excessive worrying and fear, changes in eating habits, extreme mood changes including feelings of highs or euphoria, a shift in sleeping habits, and prolonged or strong irritability or anger.

You may also feel confused, have problems concentrating and learning, have problems relating to other people, feel excessively low and sad, have a lack interest in sex, and have difficulty perceiving reality. Other symptoms include:

- Multiple physical ailments, such as stomach aches, aches and pains, and headaches.
- Drugs and alcohol abuse.
- Suicidal thoughts, intense fear of weight gain, and concern about your appearance.
- No longer having the ability to perceive change in your personality and behavior.
- Inability to carry out daily activities.

Young children are not spared. Contrary to popular belief, children also experience stress at varying levels. Because kids are learning how to express their emotions and thoughts, the most obvious symptoms are behavioral. For instance, if they were good performers at school previously and have suddenly dropped in that aspect, are excessively worried and anxious, and have hyperactive behavior, this could be a sign of a budding mental health issue, stressors in the home or school, and/or lack of coping skills. Also, your child may throw tantrums, disobey you, and have aggressive behavior frequently.

If you notice these symptoms in yourself or your child, don't be afraid to seek help. It also helps to learn more about mental health. People with a history of mental illnesses in their homes, such as blood relatives who have had a mental illness, are at higher risk of receiving it themselves. Stressful situations, such as chronic financial problems and the death of a loved one, may also trigger disease. Traumatic experiences like combat, excessive use of alcohol and drugs, abuse as a child, and brain damage are leading contributors to mental health illnesses, specifically post-traumatic stress disorder (PTSD). If you suffered a mental illness before, you may "relapse," especially if you have few healthy relationships with friends and family.

Preventing mental illness is not as direct as other diseases on this list. Granted, there is no known prevention method that will work for all of them, but there are various things you can do to control stress, boost your esteem and confidence, and increase your resilience. Prevention is, therefore, directly related to symptoms.

- **Pay attention to signs**. Educate yourself on the triggers of mental illnesses and consult your therapist if you elicit some of the symptoms. If you had suffered mental illness before, it might help to continue working with your doctor depending on the mental illness you suffered.
- **Keep close contact with friends and family**. Learning to build relationships will help you have a shoulder to lean on when things get dark. Also, you will have people to socialize and interact with. Being around people helps reduce stress.
- **Deep breathing**. This is obviously becoming a cliché, but that's because breathing does help you calm down when you are anxious. Learn breathing techniques and use them whenever you feel overwhelmed. For instance, breathe in

for five seconds, hold your breath for three, then breathe
out for seven.

- **Take care of yourself**. This includes eating nutritious food,
  avoiding tobacco, drinking a lot of water, and working out.
  Also, invest in quality sleep, since lack of sleep can
  contribute to fatigue, anxiety, and depression.
- **Give**. There is always something good that comes from
  giving, even when it's just your time and energy. Feeling
  good about doing something for someone in need is a great
  way to meet new people, have fun, and refrain from
  negative thoughts—volunteer at the homeless shelter, local
  hospital, or animal shelter.

There are many more illnesses that people suffer from, but statistics
have shown that the ones listed are the top five. Interestingly, not
many people suffered from lifestyle diseases centuries ago. In fact, the
change in diet is credited to the level of obesity and other lifestyle
diseases we now have frequently today. We have also become much less
active since jobs moved from the farm to an office setting.

Centuries ago, people used to die more to infections than they did
chronic conditions. Their diets were mainly vegetables with little to no
sugar, and the hard work they had to endure at the farm made sure
they worked out well enough for the day. As civilization and technology shifted and improved efficiency, diet changed and people
started eating more saturated fats and sugar. Thus, the rise in lifestyle
diseases.

We cannot change technology or wish we lived in the 16th century,
but we *can* choose the food we place on our table and how much time
we spend working out. With the busy lives we have today, time to work
out and go to the market for fresh produce are becoming hard nuts to
crack. Some people today hold more than two jobs and work for more
than 40 hours a week just to pay bills and enjoy a little indulgence, like
travel. We are also caught up trying to give our kids a headstart in life,
which means we want to work as hard as we can, so they can attend
better schools and have the chance to participate in better activities.

Also, the soil has been depleted so much that the food we eat doesn't have enough nutrients to supply what the body needs to remain healthy and strong. Research has shown that even eating a healthy diet is not enough, which is why so many people are turning to supplements to bridge this gap. This is especially true for older adults, but younger people are not spared either. The typical diet is highly processed and full of preservatives and sugar, which means it has little to no value in our bodies.

But, deep down, all we want is a relaxed, healthy life where we have enough time for friends and family, travel, and a career we care about. This is the "dream life" that people are after when they join a network marketing company. We have been raised to believe that we can't have it all—that we have to choose between living a "great" life by having enough money to do whatever we want or the chance to spend time with our families but struggle financially. By starting a home business, however, you work on your own terms, spend time with your family, and, if you do it well, have enough money to do the things you love.

The health and beauty industry is above a multi-billion dollar per year market. This fact has not escaped the attention of direct sale, MLM, and consumer direct companies who have no intention of being left behind. Like everyone else, they want a piece of the pie, and they are winning. Let's just take the beauty industry—the average spending for women from the neck up is around $3800 per year and approximately 25% less for the guys. Over a lifetime, this can add up to some serious cash. For women, that would be a lifetime cost of $225,360. Though they were outspent by the ladies, men are also shelling out the dinero to continue looking their best. According to Groupon's figures, men on average spend about $2,928 per year, coming out to $175,680 over the course of a lifetime. *Whoa!* I can hear the gears in your head contemplating what you could do with a sum like that; perhaps pay off your mortgage or student loans, or maybe even buy that dream car? Yeah, me too.

. . .

MULTI-LEVEL MARKETING, CONSUMER DIRECT, AND REFERRAL Marketing Business Models and the Health and Beauty Industries

Multi-level marketing—commonly known as network marketing or MLM—is a form of direct selling where distributors sell products and services, often from their homes through the phone or online. Distributors are rewarded for what they sell, but they also earn a commission from the sales generated from those in their organization or customer database (different companies call these organizations by many names). This model is such that distributors (marketers and representatives) are compensated through multiple levels of people associated in some way with them. It could be through the purchase of products or by sponsoring/recruiting them into the company. By helping, teaching, and training them to do the same as you, the company would pay you a commission on their efforts.

It's estimated that at least 10.3 million people worked in the MLM industry in 2015, retailing to about $183.7 billion. As of 2018, there are close to 20 million distributors in America retailing close to $36 billion each year. From this income, nutrition and supplements are the most popular niche types in the industry, with beauty coming in at a close second. Today, the dietary and supplement market is worth more, with an estimated increase to $230.7 billion by 2027. Companies in the health and nutrition niche are said to have contributed 35% of sales in the industry in 2016.

The majority of sales came from wellness products, centered on weight control, disinfectant cleaners, and air purifiers. The companies often claim a wide range of nutrition and health benefits from their products. These benefits maximize people's craze over fitness, immunity improvement, vitality of organs, anti-aging, and metabolism. Also, there is the issue of earning extra money, and with economic instability cycles occurring every so often, millions started looking for an additional income stream to insulate themselves from their impacts.

Think about it—if you are overweight, immobile, broke, and alone, you may desire to lose weight, so you can move around and hustle. However, when you have the option of doing it all at home through taking a few supplements and distributing the same, you may think you are set for life. A little dramatic, but you get the point. It, in fact, seems both easy and the best deal.

On the other hand, before you jump on the first network marketing train you see, I have to warn you; some companies in the direct selling industry are not always truthful. According to Truth in Advertising, the network marketing watchdog, most of the companies selling nutrition and supplements products claimed their products could heal diseases and illnesses either directly in their advertising or indirectly through their distributors. Some companies also claimed that their products could alleviate symptoms or reduce risks to diseases and disorders.

This is what has raised eyebrows, especially among members of the medical field. There is also a thin line between MLM and pyramid schemes, which is a considerable concern for people looking to join the industry.

This all begs the question: are direct sales companies legal?

The simple answer is yes; however, in truth, it's a little more complicated than that. In 1934, the first network marketing company originated in California, which sold vitamins. The company and model exploded in the rest of the world. During those days, however, distributors were keen to sell products legally by following conditions stipulated by companies like The Federal Trade Commission (FTC), which is the organization that regulates MLM businesses. Today, some companies cannot be said to follow the conditions entirely, which has brought a massive discrepancy between genuine MLMs and pyramid schemes.

To shed some light on this "grey area," let's first define what constitutes a pyramid or Ponzi scheme.

According to HowStuffWorks, a famous type of pyramid scheme is known as the "gifting scheme." In a gifting scheme, or a naked pyramid scheme, participants would "buy-in" with a set amount of money, usually donated to the person who recruited them. The participants would then recruit others to join. As more people enter the program, the participant would move up the "pyramid." In most cases, the recruiters are also promised a lump sum when they reach peak levels.

HowStuffWorks defines a Ponzi scheme as a fraudulent investment plan in which the money isn't invested. Instead, earlier participants are paid off using the money from new participants' money that gets injected into the scheme. Ponzi schemes originated in 1920 when Charles Ponzi ran the first scam. In the scheme, he promised New Englanders a 50% rate of return in just 45 days. He collected $10 million from the fraud and only paid back $8 million, keeping the difference.

Granted, there is a slight similarity between pyramid schemes and network marketing. Both have a provision where participants can recruit others. Pyramid schemes, like Ponzi schemes, only depend on recruitment as the primary source of income. The model is such that the only way to sustain the "business" is to continue recruiting more people. Participants at peak levels expect a large payout, and as more people reach these levels, the amount collected from new recruits becomes insufficient. Without the money, the scheme collapses.

In fact, pyramids only work because people lose money. If you join one, you may need ten people to recoup your investment. Those ten would then also need to bring in ten more people each, and by the eighth level, the scheme would need *one billion* recruits to remain sustainable. The next level would need 10 billion people, which is higher than the earth's population. This business model simply cannot work.

Although schemes depend on recruits for sustainability, the direct sales/MLM industry relies on selling products and services to survive. MLMs compensate distributors for the sale of products to the consumers and not merely for recruiting people. Although people earn commissions from the sales of those they recruit, the commissions are dependent on the products that the distributors purchase from the company. There has been such bad press for so long—though some of it justified—that the distinction for many people is not easy to identify.

You see, joining an MLM requires little to no investment, but buying inventory can require a considerable investment, depending on the company. And, according to the model, a distributor must first purchase the product before selling. If a distributor is unable to sell the products, they would suffer a "loss." This cost or loss makes some distributors concentrate on recruiting people instead of selling products, which can paint a genuine company as a pyramid scheme.

There can also be the issue of a "starter kit." Some companies require distributors to purchase inventory, then continue to order a monthly minimum for personal or selling purposes to qualify for commissions. These requirements can cause some distributors to think that they can make a profit by selling products to people who want them, but if they hope to make "real" money, they should concentrate on recruiting others, so they can qualify for the incentives that bringing in others entails, thus building a salesforce for the parent company.

When this happens, the line between MLMs and pyramid schemes can get a bit thin. However, when the right structure is followed, the network marketing and MLM business model can become the answer that some are looking for to stay healthy and earn some extra income.

WHY ARE DIETARY SUPPLEMENTS SO POPULAR IN MLM?

Obsessed with youth and vitality? Half of all US adults use dietary supplements, primarily to promote overall health and wellness and fill nutritional gaps. The most frequently consumed supplements include vitamins and minerals, special supplements, such as omega-3 fatty acids, enzymes, and supplements to manage symptoms caused by hormonal changes. Other popular supplements include antioxidants, botanical herbs, and sports supplements like protein formulas, amino acids, fat burners, and more.

In Europe, priority supplements differ from country to country. In France, 15.8% of adults consume supplements, mostly to fight fatigue, specific diseases, and improve overall health and wellness. These reasons, combined with the need to live healthier lives and shun the lifestyle diseases we discussed earlier, have caused the nutrition industry to explode. Dietary supplements can be sold in a powder, liquid, or capsule form. Without a doubt, energy and weight management will remain dominant through the increase in retail sales in the coming years, as awareness continues to increase, and focus shifts to nutrition and health.

In addition, here's how supplement use breaks down across the generations: millennials, currently the largest segment of society, are captivated with social media and their profile (notice all the photo filters?). Gen X'ers and boomers are vehement about keeping aging and age-related conditions at bay while they watch their parents enter an advanced age. 70% of millennials are said to use dietary supplements according to a 2016 report by the Council for Responsible Nutrition. Gen X'ers and boomers come in close at 67%.

Obesity, as we have discussed, is not only an epidemic, but it is showing up in children at younger ages. Changes in our healthcare system, rising costs of care, and lagging faith in our system have left people searching for options to take their health into their own hands in numbers larger than ever before.

In addition to the health benefits of high quality and effective vitamins and supplements offered by consumer direct and direct sales companies, there is income to consider. People are looking for ways to create an additional stream of income, and as many as 185,000 people per week look for work from home and home business opportunities. The old school method of birth, school, going to college, finding a good job, and working at the same company for 35-40 years, then retiring with a gold watch and a pension is long gone. The gig economy isn't going anywhere, and almost no-one achieves their dream retirement lifestyle with a sufficient stash of cash to sail off into the sunset.

CHAPTER SUMMARY

In this chapter, we have talked about the importance of health and nutrition and how it's related to the MLM industry. We touched on:

- The rise in sensitivity in health has spearheaded the rise in the nutrition and health industries.
- The top five health issues in America include heart disease, cancer, diabetes, kidney disease, and mental health.

- Lifestyle diseases can be prevented by everyday actions, such as eating a healthy diet, increasing your activity level several times per week, and getting enough sleep.
- The multi-level marketing, network marketing, and referral-based industry has a retail projection of $230.7 million.
- Nutritional supplements are consumed by over 50% of the population and spans across all generations.

In the next chapter, you will learn all about the eco-friendly movement and why it's becoming a $1 trillion industry.

CHAPTER FOUR: THE BUSINESS BEHIND ENVIRONMENTAL AWARENESS. THE NEXT $1 TRILLION INDUSTRY HAS ARRIVED

"By its very nature and design, network marketing is a strikingly fair, democratic, socially responsible system of generating wealth."

— ROBERT KIYOSAKI

HISTORY IS FULL OF WRONGDOINGS. HUMAN BEINGS ARE familiar with racial injustice, class exploitation, oppression, colonialism, imperialism, and sexual inequality. The historical injustices have had long-lasting effects, many of which are still present today. However, there is one form of crime that has only come into the limelight in recent years: what we have done to the environment.

In our minds, nature is limitless and cannot be depleted, but with the rate at which we are affecting the environment today, we must have learned that this is not the case. We are, in fact, eating away at the very system that sustains us. The environment has always taken a back seat, ignored and taken for granted. Activities that damage the environment are accepted as harmless when introduced on a small scale. These "small-scale introductions" have led to the problems we have today.

Small-scale degradation has led to destructive magnitudes and grown to impressive disproportions in the name of development and human advancements. However, the environment affects our health in two significant ways—first, we are affected directly through exposure to harmful agents and indirectly through the disruption of the life-sustaining ecosystem that we rely on, even without our knowledge.

Environmental degradation refers to the destruction of ecosystems and extinction of wildlife. According to the National Academies of Science, Engineering, and Medicine, ecological degradation is one of the top ten threats we need to be highly cautious of. The organization defines degradation as the "reduction of the capacity of the environment to meet social and ecological objectives and needs."

Although we approach environmental awareness from different directions and beliefs, no matter what worldview you align yourself with, most would agree that we have an obligation to take care of the planet we all call home. For instance, those in mainstream academia look at our environmental problems through a different and sometimes controversial lens. Those with a faith-based worldview believe that we have a duty to be good stewards of God's creation, and our responsibility to care for it is undeniable. Although not all faith-based groups are concerned with the environment, some are active environmentalists who promote awareness and action within the church. That is why you may see church events centered around planting trees and removing trash from hiking trails.

Environmental activists and developing countries also agree that the environment needs our urgent care. Governments in developing countries are, for example, encouraging people to plant more trees, working to reduce carbon footprints, and taking care of landfills however they can. According to CEO Magazine, Ethiopia planted 353 million trees in 2019 in different locations. Some countries have even banned the use of plastic bags because they are non-degradable, all in a bid to care more for the environment.

As far as the environment goes, life species require substantial areas to provide food, assets, and living space. This is referred to as area-specific, but since human beings have taken it too far, animals are left to scramble for the little that's left for survival. Although the environment will go on, plant life and animals are not there to help with sustainability, which is where the danger started.

Causes of Environmental Degradation

Unlike other species, we tend to leave visible scars and remains after we have depleted the earth's resources. Satellite pictures of major forests, such as the Amazon, have shown just how much we have damaged the planet. These scars are a result of the following human activities.

1. Land Degradation

The soil is the earth's fragile skin; it anchors life on earth and is composed of countless species, creating a dynamic ecosystem precious for all, especially man. Soil provides plants with the foothold they need for their roots to consume and hold necessary nutrients. It filters rainwater, regulates the discharge of excess water in the ground, and prevents flooding. It's responsible for storing large amounts of organic carbon, buffers against pollutants, and even protects groundwater, thus it remains pure and of high quality.

In short, the soil provides us with the essential construction materials we need to manufacture, including building materials, that cup of coffee you can't do without, and the food on your table. Your well-manicured lawn would not be what it is without soil, and neither would the water you use at home.

Soil degradation is a result of erosion, whether it's through agriculture or deforestation. In the past, human beings relied on natural vegetation for their meals, but the transition to agriculture on a large scale and the introduction of GMO plants have led to a new set of issues with regard to our food supply. This includes common plants such as soybeans, cotton, wheat, coffee, and palm oil. This transition has led to erosion, to a point where the soil has become unable to maintain itself.

Interestingly, half of the soil on the planet has been here for more than 150 years, but the quality has been affected by many agricultural aspects; for instance, soil structure has changed, nutrients have been depleted, and soil salinity and compaction have all been negatively affected. Obviously, this is a concern for farmers and the global community because our collective livelihood depends on the soil.

Soil degradation is a result of the use of agrochemicals, overgrazing, and deforestation. Although these have caused the majority of the deterioration we see today, other factors are mostly not mentioned. For instance, copper mines in Jordan, Faynan showed that copper was smelted there more than 3000 years ago during the reign of King Solomon. The Tonglu Mountain copper mines in China are also another incident that caused huge soil degradation. The 28-kilometer mountain has mining pits as old as 2000-3000 years old, dated back to the Western Zhou and Han dynasties. On-site, you can find waste remains from the mining site. Swaziland also has mines dating back thousands of years, whose activity still affects our world today. The deserts of Mesopotamia is another example. Traditionally, modern Iraq was a Mesopotamian landscape with agriculturally rich Fertile Crescent turned into dry landscapes and salty marshlands.

Egypt—the world's oldest civilization—is also said to have contributed a lot to the world's environment today. The beautiful pyramids of Giza that are a sight to behold left unimaginable scars on the soil. Scientists in 1993 uncovered a 28-kilometer stretch of road running through the southwestern desert of Cairo covered in sandstones, petrified wood, and limestone, dating back 4,600 years. Although it's fascinating to imagine that paved roads are not new, it's also saddening to imagine the scars this left on our precious earth.

War is also another culprit that's rarely talked about. When we think about war, suffering, pain, violence, and triumph are probably what comes to mind because of the immediate human impact. We hold vigils for those who lost their lives during large-scale wars and compensate families of fallen soldiers in an attempt to mitigate suffering. We, however, hardly mention the impact the war has had on the environment. Because of this, the effects are hardly recognizable.

Pearl Harbor, for instance, still evokes emotions in every American when we remember how our grandparents struggled against the Japanese during WWII. However, when you visit USS Arizona, you may notice the brightly colored oil that has been slowly leaking from the wreck since its sinking. It's said that over 5000 gallons of oil remain, and scientists warn that a sudden spill would be disastrous.

The Rwandan civil war and genocide are not news—especially since most of us witnessed it—but nobody talks about the environmental impact it had. In part, the genocide was spurred by a lack of resources as people tried to lift themselves from poverty, thus exploiting the forest and wildlife. As deforestation and wildlife exploitation increased, instability in the economy grew, resources became unstable, and tension heightened. The genocide created an influx in refugees, extinction of wildlife, and reduced resources that would take years to recover.

During times of war, it's common for human beings to take cover in the forest, which is what happened in Vietnam. It worked until the US started using herbicide, or the famous "Agent Orange," to kill off massive forest growth to fish out guerilla fighters. This caused direct harm to the environment, affected the ecosystem, and impacted the health of Vietnamese people and American soldiers alike. Congenital disabilities, rashes, tumors, and an increase in cancer were and are some of the effects of Agent Orange.

2. Pollution

Whatever form it takes—air, land, noise, or water—pollution is harmful to the environment. Air pollution, for instance, is one of the most common causes of environmental degradation. It introduces contaminants into the environment that can maim and kill plants and animals. Automobiles and industries are the main contributors to air pollution, and it was estimated to cause at least two million premature deaths in the world in 1997. Today, the World Health Organization says that approximately 4.2 million deaths occur each year due to exposure to outdoor air pollution. Therefore, reducing air pollution will reduce respiratory illnesses, lung cancer, and even heart disease.

For every gallon of gasoline that is manufactured, distributed, and burned by vehicles, 25 pounds of carbon dioxide is produced and released into the air. This is alongside carbon monoxide, nitrogen dioxide, and sulfur dioxide, and it is why damping chemicals, plastics, and other waste products will continue to plague the earth.

The European Environment Agency also said that 77% of people living in urban areas in Europe are exposed to air quality levels that exceed a concentration safe for human beings. This is the same case with 90% of the urban population in Turkey according to research published in a journal by the Maharishi Arvind College of Engineering and Technology. Low- and middle-income countries suffer more from exposure, both indoors and outdoors. Air pollution is also linked to higher heart disease rates, cancer, stroke, and respiratory illnesses such as asthma. In America alone, at least 134 million people are at risk of contracting a disease of premature death credited to air pollution. This is according to estimates by the American Lung Association.

The best example of water pollution are the images we see on social media of fish fighting to get plastic bags off their necks or turtle's fins trapped on plastic. You will find tons of garbage, chemicals, and other pollutants across all bodies of water, such that 80% of the world's water is polluted. Though largely untreated, this water is taken back into the environment, lakes, rivers, and oceans. This is the same water that some people will use to cook, clean, and drink.

Unfortunately, unsafe water kills more people than war and all other forms of violence combined. The Bureau of Reclamation says that only 3% of the world's water is fresh water; yet, the entire world drinks less than 1% of the water found on earth. This is according to Mike Malina in his book *Delivering Sustainable Buildings: An industry insider's view.* The demand for freshwater expands by one-third, which will create a massive challenge by 2050. It's shocking to learn that 40% of the world's water is not fit for swimming or fishing. In addition, the mercury in fish is higher today than it has ever been before.

Water is unique, in that it's a universal solvent. This means that water dissolves more substance than any other liquid available, but that's also why it's so easily polluted. Toxins from farms, factories, and towns can dissolve and mix with water easily, causing pollution. Groundwater is the most critical natural resource, and nearly 40% of the United States relies on it for drinking water. Some people in rural areas rely solely on groundwater as a source of freshwater. When groundwater mixes with fertilizers and pesticides from our farms, it renders the water unsafe.

Surface water, which covers 70% of the earth's water, has not been spared. Lakes, oceans, and rivers account for 60% of surface water, but most of it is polluted. One-third of lake water, for instance, is contaminated with traces of phosphates and nitrates—the leading contaminants in water. Plants and animals need these nutrients to grow, but when in excess, they can become major pollutants, mainly due to farm waste and fertilizers. The municipal and industrial waste also contribute, not counting the random junk that individuals and industries dump directly into the water.

The environment has many sounds, from rustling leaves (20 to 30 decibels) to thunderclaps (120 decibels). Sounds higher than 85 decibels hurt the ears, yet we have grown accustomed to listening to these high-frequency sounds. For instance, a home lawnmower is 90 decibels, while the subway is between 90 and 115 decibels. The music concerts we love to attend can be anywhere between 110 to 120 decibels. This is noise pollution.

The most common health problem from noise pollution is Noise Induced Hearing Loss (NIHL). It also causes sleep disturbance, stress, heart disease, and high blood pressure. Children are most affected by noise pollution. Humans are not the only ones affected. According to National Geographic, ships and oil drills have made the once tranquil seas environment chaotic, impacting whales and dolphins the most. Also, noise pollution causes the heart of caterpillars to beat faster and bluebirds to have fewer chicks. These animals use echolocation to communicate, feed, find mates, and navigate. The interference from noise makes this impossible, affecting their survival.

Lastly, landfills pollute the environment and destroy the beauty of our cities. A large amount of waste we see is brought about by our home, factories, hospitals, and industries. The landfills pose a considerable risk to our health, especially for people who live close to them.

Undoubtedly, you have heard the above pollution scenarios, but have you ever considered the inside of your home as part of the environment? According to the Environmental Protection Agency, the top five air quality problems in the U.S. are all indoor air problems—

viruses, bacteria, and pesticides, just to name a few. And, according to the Center for Disease Control, over 300 children in the United States between ages 0 to 19 are rushed to the emergency room every day. Two kids are said to die of poisoning daily.

Chemicals with clear warning labels are dangerous to children, but they are not the only ones you need to be careful about. Items such as household cleaners and medicines also pose a health risk because they are often poisonous to kids. People are becoming more aware of what they're bringing into their home, not only for their children's wellbeing, but also theirs and their pets'. There are several eco-friendly products available through companies that employ the MLM/direct sales business model. Through their reps' marketing efforts, these companies are largely responsible for the shift in consumers' demand for safer products.

THE BUSINESS BEHIND ENVIRONMENTAL AWARENESS

It's only been a few years since companies started making efforts to go green. Think about the coffee you enjoy in the morning—the paper cup you use is recyclable and so is metal and many more types of materials today. Although it may have looked like a fad in the beginning, businesses large and small are genuinely interested in caring for the environment.

The push may have come from people becoming more sensitive to the environmental impact businesses have because, according to the reports and research done by Engine Insight, 80% of people respect and prefer working with a brand that adopts eco-friendly practices.

Companies that go green are focused on two things: they want to make a profit, but they want to do it while having a negligible impact on the environment, and in some cases, benefit the environment. This means that sustainability becomes a key consideration within the company and steers decision making; for instance, it could influence the materials they use in the production of their products, which can include the use of chemicals that have a reduced effect on the environment. We have seen this in recent years in the bottled water industry with the reduction of plastic used in companies' bottles, and an increase in recyclable materials elsewhere.

By recognizing the dwindling nature of our planet, businesses are working steadily to ensure they help mother-nature as much as possible. Going green manifests itself in different ways, depending on the business. For instance, some companies capitalize on saving energy by installing solar panels. At the same time, your local restaurant may use a bike to make deliveries within the neighborhood to reduce emissions. Whichever efforts they make, several advantages come with going green.

- **It saves the company money**

Going green costs some money upfront. If you think of installing solar panels, for example, you have to part with a substantial amount to make it happen for your residence. Now, scale that up to industry level, and you can see how costs will rise. However, eventually, the company will gain more by taking these green measures.

Besides solar panels, companies install LED lights to save more in the long run because the bulbs last at least forty times longer while using one-tenth of the energy that an incandescent bulb uses. This, combined with solar panels, is a huge save for the company. Fossil fuel prices are expected to increase, but as technology advances, solar panels and prices for them will continue to become more competitive. This "price exchange" in itself helps in steering companies toward using greener options.

- **Consumers love green companies**

As we've already discussed, 80% of consumers prefer to work with companies that care for the environment. A while back, all a company had to do was advertise themselves as green companies, and consumers would back them up. The ads have gone down recently because, as technology has advanced, consumers have learned to evaluate just how green a company is.

The supply chain of an organization is online, where it's accessible to anyone—of that information, the company's energy use and emissions are also available. With this forced transparency, businesses now have to go green because under the watchful eyes of the consumers, going green wins consumer brand loyalty, expands the company's market share, and increases profits.

- **Stimulates innovation**

It's easy to fall into a comfort zone, even for companies; however, issues like environmental conservancy triggers innovation. Companies are, thus, forced to think of whether the processes they have are the best, most efficient, or most effective solutions. This forces organizations to always be on the lookout for ways to save money and become more efficient, all while saving the environment.

Delivery routes become optimized to save energy and lower carbon emissions, and the manufacturing processes become streamlined to save time, energy, and reduce air pollution. Also, less bulky packaging and sometimes even a change in packaging materials ensures the use of environmentally friendly materials.

- **Helps the environment**

This is the ultimate goal of going green, and although repeating it may seem redundant, it's worth mentioning. Without a doubt, reducing emissions reduces environmental degradation, and even in the slightest way, it can help the earth start healing. By protecting the natural habitats and ecosystems, we protect our very livelihood and ensure that we have a safe, healthy place for future generations.

THE $1 TRILLION INDUSTRY

As the population grows and access to resources reduces, people are becoming increasingly sensitive and open to using less harmful products. This sensitivity and use is increased if the products are easy to find and use compared to what they are already used to. Consumers are even willing to pay higher for products made by environmentally friendly companies. Some studies have also shown that at least 71% of Americans consider the environment as a factor when they shop—no wonder the organic food sales have skyrocketed!

A study by Lucien Georgeson said that the green economy—as it has come to be known—generates approximately $1.3 trillion a year and employs close to 9.5 million full-time employees. While $1.3 trillion caters to only 7% of the country's GDP, the impact it has on the environment cannot be refuted. And that's good news; we are making progress.

Individuals also have a role to play in reducing energy use and recycling their waste and helping eco-friendly companies work hard to make a difference. That's why people are installing solar panels, switching to LED bulbs at home, and buying from brands that help the earth. Likewise, businesses are gaining the foothold they need to grow and thrive in a changing economy as more people prefer green products.

The sensitivity to a green economy will not end. As time moves forward, people will only find more reasons to adapt to using products and services from an organization that cares about the environment. Even the direct sales industry is aware of this fact.

Perhaps the most significant advantage you have as a distributor, marketing executive, or representative is the opportunity to work with a company whose vision, mission, and products you believe in. In addition, with the rise of the green economy, it makes sense to align oneself with a company that caters to and cares about the environment, not just because statistics support that consumers purchase from companies that care for the environment, but because everyone has to play a role.

Many direct sales, consumer direct marketing, and MLM companies were founded by people who were deeply tied to their vision and goal of sustainability and designed and formulated effective products using biodegradable ingredients. They brought them to the marketplace to compete with corporate giants and were successful. Their business model just so happens to create literally a wealth of opportunity for those who share their views.

Companies that operate with this type of business model offer you a unique path to financial freedom by building a business around a company and products that interest you. They also provide an alternative to traditional corporate jobs and workplaces, which, in the world we live in, gives you a chance to work from anywhere and at any time. However, like other businesses, you will find companies that use "greenwash" when marketing their products.

Greenwash refers to companies that spend time advertising their products and services as green, environmentally friendly, or organic. Still, if you look closely, their processes aren't actually doing the environment any favors. In some cases, even the products themselves have little to no positive effect on the environment. Instead, companies capitalize on public relations and advertising to take advantage of gullible people who won't do their own research on whether a company is really green before they buy.

As mentioned, this is a problem that cuts across the board. It is imperative to do your own research and choose a company that genuinely cares about the environment when considering your options. With all the pollution we have today, the earth could use all the help we can offer in order to sustain ecosystems and ensure we have a place to live in.

Most people are attracted to network marketing because of the opportunity to generate an additional income stream, create a lifestyle that has more time freedom, support the family, and work from the ground up on something they believe in. However, it's absolutely vital that you draw the line between recruiting and making money, and help people make healthier choices to live better lives.

Although companies may be quick to tell you that they are taking care of the environment, you need to take a closer look and figure out if their claims are true. With network marketing, you can have it all. Position yourself with an established brand, profit from promoting their products, expand your social circle, spend more time with your family, and care for the environment while you're at it.

Chapter Summary
In this chapter, we talked about:

- The causes of environmental degradation such as pollution, land degradation, and natural causes.
- Consumers are becoming more aware of pollutants inside the home and are demanding safer and more natural products.
- More companies are going green today, as they recognize the role they play in harming the environment.
- 80% of consumers prefer to buy with companies that are environmentally conscious and have a green policy in place.
- Consumers consider eco-friendliness a major factor when buying goods and services.
- Environmentally friendly businesses are worth at least $1.3 trillion, which accounts for 7% of the country's GDP.
- By aligning yourself with an MLM company with eco-friendly policies, you can profit from promoting their products while spending more with your family and earning an income.

In the next chapter, you will learn about the concept of consumer connectedness and why multi-level marketing companies are winning at it.

CHAPTER FIVE: CUSTOMER CONNECTEDNESS

Multi-level, or network marketing, is an excellent second income opportunity. Millions of people all over America and throughout the world are taking advantage of the opportunity multi-level marketing offers to start and build a successful business, quickly and inexpensively. They use the foundation of a network marketing business to learn vital business skills at a low cost."

— BRIAN TRACY

IN CHAPTER ONE, WE TALKED ABOUT HOW TECHNOLOGY HAS changed the business world and touched on some of the things it has helped customers and businesses with. One of the major things we need to look at in detail are the connection and relationship that technology has helped build.

In the past, you were only able to reach a company with a complaint if you went to their offices, wrote to them, or called them. You had no way of building a relationship with the company, and what they said was final. Most complaints were just that, complaints that no one did anything about. Fast forward to when the internet started gaining momentum, and you could now send the company an email.

Customer service improved slightly, but power was still in the hands of the business. They could choose to ignore your email no matter how often you complained, or they could hide vital information from you, and there would be nothing you could do. Today, however, that has changed.

A simple click of a button could mean bashing a company online and destroying its reputation within minutes. Companies are more careful when interacting with you and are more professional and "human." They are no longer far off, but as close as your mobile phone. You can chat with a customer representative and have your query answered in real time. If you aren't satisfied, a company that is interested in its reputation will go to great lengths to ensure you get the best service possible.

Also, you have the power to post reviews about a company's performance on numerous online platforms. This keeps the company on their toes, and they would seek to deliver top-notch service for that glowing five-star review. Power is now finally in your hands.

But what has this shift in power changed in terms of how companies operate? Does it come with any benefits?

To answer this question accurately, let's think about the owner of the business first. When starting a business, one of the first things on their minds is becoming profitable quickly. They want to survive amidst stiff competition, and they must always strive to come up with ways to grow and expand. One of the best channels to use for this purpose is technology and how it affects business operations—not just in terms of creating efficiency and accuracy, but in learning about the customers and understanding their needs.

Technology, for instance, is at the forefront of decreased customer attention. The availability of millions of blogs and videos has become an information-overload. In a single day, you will have tons of videos to watch, numerous emails to answer, and too much to accomplish at your job, which may sometimes require you to read a few blogs or articles, answer coworkers, or interact with customers. The time you give each task decreases significantly, which makes grabbing a reader's attention and retaining it crucial for success in business.

Companies have thus sought to be helpful as opposed to pushing products and services. They would rather give you valuable information and keep you longer on their sites, slowly establishing themselves as an authority in the subject. Authority builds trust, and once you trust a company, you will be more likely to buy their goods and services.

Because people spend so much time online, they crave personal interaction as opposed to talking to bots. That's why you may accept a piece of content that reads like it was written for you and shun one that sounds like a robot wrote it. Personalization of each message has become a huge determinant of the consumer's experience when people visit a company's site. It's so important that a study was conducted by Janrain to find why people leave websites even when the content is useful. According to the results published, 74% of online users like you and I feel frustrated when a site is full of pop-ups, promotional offers, and ads, especially when they have nothing to do with what took you to the site in the first place.

Businesses are thus creating content that's tailor-made for your needs, recommending products that you are interested in while keeping anything annoying out of your browser. This makes it easier to purchase products because you found exactly what you were looking for.

You also expect excellent customer service. Previously, you probably bought a product or used a service regardless of how it made you feel. It was more about just finding something that would suffice. But today, if you experience horrible customer service or a company makes you feel dissatisfied, angry, or bad during the purchase process, you are likely to walk away and never look back.

A report posted by RightNow showed that 89% of customers will stop doing business with a company after experiencing poor customer service. That's how important customer service is today and how much people expect it. Perhaps the most crucial benefit technology has brought to both companies and customers is the ability to build brand trust and likability.

Let's think for a moment about your best friend—if they called you in the middle of the day and told you to open the door, you would most likely comply without question. You simply trust that there is something great or at least entertaining waiting for you on the other end.

Now, companies do not have the luxury of becoming your best friend; however, if they can build trust and connect with you, they stand a better chance of retaining you as a customer. You will likely, in turn, continue giving them repeat business because you trust them in a similar way to how you would trust your best friend. Dimensional Research found that 90% of customers said that positive reviews impacted their buying decision, while also citing that these positive reviews made them buy products from a company. The same goes for negative reviews—85% of customers admitted that they didn't purchase because the company had negative reviews.

Since customer connectedness and trust are so vital, precisely what are they, and how do companies build and use them?

Customer Connectedness

A while back, I was having lunch with a friend, and she had just ordered cleaning products for her house from a new company. For some reason, she could not stop talking about how well the company had treated her.

What shocked her the most was that someone had answered the phone on the second ring. No bots were telling her to press a specific number to speak to someone, or to have a particular need met. Instead, she called and someone answered. No automated greetings or anything of the sort.

We have to admit that rarely happens.

When her shock wore off, she asked the representative to place an order of the products she needed. Three minutes into the call and my friend knew how long it would take to get her cleaning products, how much it will cost, and the representative wanted to know if there was anything else she could help her with.

Now, my friend can't stop talking about how awesome the

company is. Her feelings about the company changed in three minutes, and she went from trusting them to becoming a company advocate.

On a similar note, let's imagine you are feeling thirsty and looking for something to quench your thirst. Walking down the aisle of a store, your mind is probably thinking of only one red and white can. Whether it's the carbonated bubbles, aluminum cracking, or sweet taste you feel when you drink it, there is no doubt there's an emotional connection between you and the drink.

This emotional connection is what steers us toward brand loyalty.

How Emotions Influence Customer Connectedness

Zig Ziglar once said that "people don't buy for logical reasons. They buy for emotional reasons."

Gerald Zaltman, a Harvard professor in his book *How Customers Think: Essential Insights into the Minds of the Market*, reveals that you are probably not as savvy as you may think when making a purchase decision.

Let's assume you need a new phone. You spend days researching different brands, specs, and all that shenanigans. Within a few days, you make a choice and head to the shop to pick up your phone. According to Zaltman, your unconscious physical reactions—what you think and say—often contradict each other. Unconscious urges—the biggest being your emotions—determine why you would choose a particular product over another.

There are various reasons why you, like my friend, would connect emotionally to a brand. For instance, you may have grown up knowing a particular detergent was the best because, as you watched your favorite TV show as a kid, the ads would always appear during each break. You may have also used a particular product because someone you considered a role model in your family used that product. Maybe you are still with the bank that your parents had you using, or you eat that sugary cereal because your favorite aunt bought it for you when you first went over for a sleepover.

Like my friend, you may feel connected to a brand because of the personal touch in their service. The ultimate customer experience is something we all seem to crave today. All this seems to suggest one thing: an emotional connection with customers is just as valuable as a highly satisfied buyer. You never seem to consider the price when you connect with a business on an emotional level, and you may even buy more products and services than you intended to.

But how do businesses connect with you on that emotional level? Frankly, nobody really knows for sure because there are psychological, emotional, and cultural patterns that influence all of us. In other words, there is no hard and fast rule on why people connect emotionally with brands. However, that doesn't mean science doesn't have an explanation.

NET EMOTIONAL VALUE

Companies first seek to understand your Net Emotional Value. Net Emotional Value (NEV) states that twenty emotions can drive or destroy any company. They are classified into four major clusters. These are:

- **Advocacy**—Where you feel happy and pleased with the company. That's why you will always reach for a red and white can of soda and not a blue and white one, or why you prefer one box or cereal over another.
- **Recommendation**—You feel like you trust and value a brand. You care about them and believe that they also care about you.
- **Attention**—You feel interested in the company's products and services. You may even feel stimulated, indulgent, and exploratory, wanting to know more about them and the service they offer.
- **Destroying**—As the name suggests, you feel like you could ruin the brand because you are irritated, unhappy, stressed, frustrated, disappointed, hurried, or neglected.

Every interaction you have with a business will cultivate either positive or negative emotions. The more a company can steer you toward positive emotions, the better your experience will be, and the stronger the emotional connection. So, a company needs to do several things to attain a positive emotional connection with you.

1. Understand a Customer's Emotional Drive

A company will spend time thinking about what makes you happy, then tailor their marketing in a way that shows you they get you and will help you get the feeling you are after. If you notice soda ads, they will often start with the cracking of aluminum as a person opens the can, then the bubbles will follow, and the oh-so-sweet taste, and, finally, the satisfaction. All this goodness—while interacting with friends and friends—would be people you trust. Seeing this ad automatically tells you that this is what you will experience when you receive your own drink, and it's even better when you share it with your inner circle.

When you visit a restaurant with friends—or are with a date you are trying to impress—you will feel disappointed when the food takes an hour to make it to the table. However, if they send the food over with a personalized apology and a bottle of wine on the side, you may automatically feel like your patronage is important to them. Things will be even better if the meal is as finger-licking as you had imagined. Because your server or the restaurant manager took the time to understand your disappointment, apologized, and made a meal worth waiting for, all would be forgiven.

2. Brands Will Tell a Story

When I was seated listening to my friend blabber about buying cleaning products, I wasn't interested in the cream per se, but in the story behind the cream and buying experience that made it worth her sharing with me. That story alone would have made me buy the cream for myself. Stories bring us together, but they also activate the emotional center in our brains. That's why you feel sad when you listen to what happened to Debbie from accounting or why you cried when you watched *The Titanic* for the first time.

That's why customer testimonials are vital in your buying journey. At the back of your mind, you know that things will work for you because they did for hundreds of others. On the other hand, a bad review may scare you away, or at least make you think twice before placing an order.

3. Interact with Customers

Remember that phone call that turned my friend into a believer? To her, the customer representative got a deeper understanding of her need, so getting out her credit card to buy wasn't a problem. That's the same thing that happens to you when you chat with a customer care representative; they listen to your predicament, offer you solutions, and, in some cases, even empathize with your situation.

This interaction will make you trust the brand more than you did, and with how they are willing to move mountains to get your situation solved builds an emotional relationship. When your emotional needs are met, you become a believer, and they develop a stronger brand.

Obviously, technology is at the forefront of ensuring brands know how you feel and how to meet your needs. Through strong social media connections, businesses interact with and learn more about you, which prompts them to stop treating you like a lead and more like the unique individual you are. They stop thinking about marketing their products and services and more about how to meet your needs to satisfy you with the service.

It sounds easy in theory, but being authentic and giving a personal touch is not a walk in the park; despite that, it's essential because followers will see right through you if your goal is to get their credit card number without caring for their needs. That's what makes network marketing so successful—this connection is deeply engraved in the business model, making it easy for others to purchase products and services. Consumer direct and referral business models are effective because each customer is linked to someone who is keenly interested in making sure they are a happy customer

Now that we understand customer connectedness, let's take a closer look at why it makes the multi-level marketing business model work.

Customer Connectedness and Multi-level Marketing

There are a few things we have already touched on about multi-level marketing, (network marketing, direct sales, and consumer direct marketing). First, it's that people who join MLMs earn an income by recommending or selling products to others through direct sales. Second is that, as a distributor, you can recruit other people to join the company, so you can earn a commission from their sales.

We also talked about the difference between a scam and an MLM, so we won't go back to that. The million-dollar questions, however, are: what makes MLM companies so successful? How is it linked to customer connectedness? A few things come to light based on how the MLM business model is constructed.

Trust and Customer Connectedness

Multi-level marketing understands and uses the same marketing principle other companies use. They know that connecting with customers is vital to growing the business. Now, if you look closely at the model used by MLMs, you will notice that many emphasize selling to the people closest to you. This includes your friends, family, and colleagues.

This group of people already trusts you and is likely to listen to you because of the close relationship you have. Let's assume you are in the beauty industry, and one of your friends compliments you, saying that your skin is glowing and your foundation works for your skin. Using a story, you could tell them how you found the company, and just like that, you could earn yourself a customer.

You have already connected with your friend, and since they trust you, you are positioned uniquely to package your product in a way that addresses a problem, want, or need. This is, however, easier said than done. Your friend may have noticed that your skin is glowing, but that doesn't mean they want to change from their current brand to what you are using.

Like buying a product from any other company, your friend may also ask relevant questions. For instance, how much does the product cost? Will the product arrive on time? Will it arrive at all? Is there a return policy? What will happen to the personal information they give you?

So, although you are their friend, you must make them feel at ease enough to abandon their current brand and purchase from you instead. That's only one side of the business—you must think about your downline (organization, team, customer database, etc.)

If a building is not set on a firm foundation, it will fall, which is the same concept with any network marketing business. You must not only establish a relationship with your clients, but also with your downline. You must invest time by keeping in touch, encouraging them, and even becoming their friend.

PERSONALIZATION AND AUTHENTICITY

Each company attempts to brand themselves in a way that communicates to its customers effectively. That's why people will line up in one store for hours, waiting for the launch of a new phone and completely ignore the other. The brand speaks to them, makes them feel like part of a movement, and meets their needs as far as phones are concerned.

Now, think about your network marketing team and the approach they use when talking to prospects. It's easy to call an old friend you haven't seen in ten years and invite them for coffee. From there, you can slowly deviate from "catching up" to talking about the amazing opportunity you have and how they can benefit. Don't get me wrong —this works to some extent, but the fact that you didn't take time to first connect with the said friend is a red flag that can send people running for the hills and never looking back. For many, this tactic reeks of desperation and rarely works long term. Authenticity and genuineness may take longer, but you will build a more solid and long-lasting business with your self-respect and reputation intact.

You are doing the same thing you hate when you are on the receiving end—that is, treating your prospects as a lead and not a person.

What if you took it easy and genuinely became interested in what was happening in their life? As you do this, observe their emotional needs and establish a connection before you even mention your products, service, or opportunity. For instance, your friend may mention how they would love to find a product that would help with eczema or natural cleaning products, but they have been unsuccessful in finding some that actually work. Find out more about their situation and what an ideal circumstance would be for them, and most of all, be honest and credible. Be prepared to court them for months, or even years; building trust, rapport, and a thriving network marketing or consumer direct marketing business is a marathon, not a sprint.

Now, use your product to meet this need. It doesn't have to be immediate, and it doesn't have to sound forced. It could be a story of how you found these amazing products and why you believe they are great. Ask your friend to read more about them, so they can learn if it's worthwhile for them. Remember to position yourself as a leader in the industry, so your friend can come to you when they're ready. It may take a little time, but when you finally send products to your friend, you will have a customer for life. Beyond that, do *not* make outrageous claims! This does not do the industry, nor anyone in it, any favors!

BELONG TO A GROUP

Human beings are social by nature—we want to belong in a group and feel that we are accepted and understood. That's why we buy from companies that "get us" or make us feel valued. The direct sales industry has taken this a notch higher because once you sign-up, you become part of the team. Each team has a leader who shows you how to build your business and offers their help whenever you need it.

A good team leader recognizes that their ability to lead, encourage, and teach impacts their income directly, so they would do whatever they can to help you prosper. If you hear an upline (sponsor or mentor) refer to their downlines (team, organization) as deadbeats and non-performers, you can be sure that those in their organization will soon drop off and leave the business for another opportunity. They will feel neglected, disappointed, frustrated, and stressed. These are the same feelings we described under the "destroying" cluster when discussing net emotional value earlier in this chapter. This applies to selling products and recruiting as well.

When a company is marketing, they recognize that people enter into the sales funnel at different points. If you remember from chapter one, we summarized these levels into three—first, there is the "trigger," where you realize you need a particular product or service. The second level is when you research the product, gathering as much information as possible. Lastly, we have the point when you finally purchase the product and decide if you like it or not after experiencing its performance.

You may get to know the company during the first or second stage, which is perfectly normal. If it's during the first stage—like most people—you would automatically go to your "default" settings and buy what you are already used to. There is no research included because you already experienced the product before. At this point, you may also be loyal to the brand because you love their service or feel an emotional connection because of the relationship you built before.

In some cases, however, you may either want to switch brands or are looking to try a new product because the one you're using no longer performs as well as it did at first, has been discontinued, or you want something different. You may have decided that the brands you have been using no longer represent your values. Remember the "attention" cluster in the net emotional value—this is where a person feels stimulated, exploratory, and interested in a brand.

During the second stage, suppose you are busy researching a product you are interested in, and suddenly, another product comes to mind or on your Facebook timeline through an ad. You hadn't thought about it, but now that you've read what the ad says, you are interested in learning more.

Next, let's employ the same concept to network marketing. In this industry, you earn by selling or referring products and through commissions from your organization's efforts. Therefore, when marketing the company, you have to recognize at which point you need to connect with the prospect you want to sell products or recruit into joining the company.

The prospect will either be at the first stage where they recognize the need they have, or the second stage where they are already researching a product or service. Let's go back to our example where a friend is interested in finding a product to help with their eczema. Assume you haven't called them for a coffee date—because you are friends on Facebook, they reach out to you about the products you have been talking about and ask for more information.

At this point, you aren't sure if they want to buy the product, are just curious, or need a specific problem solved. Your job is to, therefore, find out what your friend's need is, connect with them emotionally, and show them how your products and company are the best way to meet this need. You can do this by being authentic, asking questions, listening to their story, and presenting them with a solution.

This prospect will either be in the second phase or going back to the trigger stage because the product they were using before isn't working anymore. Whatever the case, your primary role is to listen and gather the information you can use to connect with the prospect. This doesn't mean you would become upset and treat the prospect like nothing but a lead; people hate being treated like leads, and I'm sure you don't like it either. Instead, be genuinely interested in knowing their problem, offer the person value, then position your products as something they need.

For instance, your friend may be coming to you because they are curious about choosing a foundation color for their skin tone. Perhaps they are complaining about how the company they buy from doesn't have enough shades, and they either have to use something lighter, which makes them look like a ghost, or something darker, which was not their intention.

Start by offering valuable solutions on how someone can select the right foundation shade. During your explanation, you can use your company as an example if they already provide tons of shades for people to choose from. Show the prospect how easy it is to choose from the wide range of products and the shade that will look great on them. By doing this, you warm them up and make them want to know more about your company without you appearing salesy.

If a prospect is really interested in buying from your company, they would move to the second stage, where they may have several questions while they are trying to figure out your products and why they should consider them. The customer service you offer at this point will determine if they will stick around and form an emotional connection with you and the company or run for the hills.

So, instead of telling them what a great opportunity they will have first, tell them how your product will meet their needs and let them experience it for themselves. If you love something, you will automatically want to become an advocate for it. That's why word of mouth is still the most powerful form of marketing.

Let's assume your friend buys the product, loves it, and out of the blue, they tag you on a Facebook post, giving you a glowing review of how you changed their lives with the product or service. A few of their friends may want to know more about it, but because your friend doesn't have all the information, they then ask you for help. At this point, it's natural to introduce your friend to the business. Remember that not everyone will be interested in joining, and that's ok.

The logic of consumer connectedness is not lost on network marketing, direct sales, MLM, and consumer direct companies; in fact, it is foundational to them. Nearly everything they build upon from inception to becoming a billion-dollar company is tied to it. As we already discussed, the emotional connection is paramount to the customer's buying decision and also plays a huge role in converting the initial purchase into brand loyalty and repeat business.

By employing these business models, companies and their products have already overcome the purchasing decision obstacle through their representatives. This aids the company in gaining access to their circle of influence, and thus sidestep some of the noise in the marketplace that competes for our attention. For instance, you don't have to spend hours researching a company because someone you trust already gave you a testimonial by witnessing the product or service work for them.

Let's think about that friend who lost weight and is now rocking dresses they couldn't have worn before and that other friend who couldn't stop talking about the amazing experience she had when buying cleaning products. You are very likely to want to try the products for yourself now because of the testimonials you received from your friends.

Think also of that article or Facebook post your friend tagged you on. Because it's someone you have built a connection with who tagged you, you will probably trust their judgment and check it out. This is the same concept and model that network marketing companies follow.

As a company representative, you are already advertising for them through word of mouth, so they don't need to spend thousands of dollars on TV and social media platforms. Instead, they can spend that time and money paying you great commission, motivating you, and on seminars to teach you the skills you need to be successful.

Without a doubt, the internet has broadened the market reach and helped savvy marketers overcome barriers and connect with customers from all over the world. Your next downline could be from Europe or Alaska. If you can connect with them online, you can recruit them to join your organization/team. In turn, they will sell the products and services to their friends and start their own team/organization.

Connecting with customers, no matter where they are in the world, is vital to running a business. Successful companies don't take shortcuts—they build the business on the most crucial aspect of any business: customer service. Without a doubt, that's the same model you should follow. Align yourself with a company whose products and services you love, have experienced, and feel are truly worth the value. This way, you can concentrate on connecting with prospects and building your business without worrying that the products will be a disappointment.

CHAPTER SUMMARY

The most important things we've learned in this chapter are:

- People make buying decisions emotionally, not logically.

- When interacting with a brand, people will either have positive or negative feelings.
- The more a person feels positive about your brand, the better the chances of them buying from and being loyal to you.
- Don't treat your prospects like leads—treat them like human beings to make it easier to build an emotional connection with them.
- Customer connectedness is the driving force behind great brands, and will thus be the driving force behind success as a direct sales distributor.

In chapter five, you will learn about finding a work-life balance, and how you can have both.

LET'S KEEP IN TOUCH! BECOME A SUBSCRIBER TO MY EMAIL LIST. Don't worry, I won't fill your inbox with useless fluff. I will, however, send an occasional newsletter, industry news, or free giveaways. It's easy, simply go to **cdwolfebooks.com** to sign up. Quick and painless—I promise.

CHAPTER SIX: FRUSTRATION! HOW CAN I FIND WORK LIFE BALANCE

"I am often asked if network marketing is a pyramid scheme. My reply is that corporations really are pyramid schemes. A corporation has only one person at the top, generally the CEO, and everyone else below. If I lost everything and had to start again, I would find myself a great network marketing company and get to work."

— DONALD TRUMP

WHEN YOU WERE GROWING UP, THERE WERE SOME "LUXURIES" you must have wished your parents could afford, but because of the financial circumstances, they couldn't. It could be that trip to Disneyland or a toy you wanted but couldn't have. Maybe it was even something as simple as a favorite treat. So, you worked hard at school and did your best to get into college—and now you have a good job, a beautiful house, and a great family.

You can finally afford that trip to Disneyland, never stress about a meal out or that trip to the grocery store, and you can spoil your kids with toys. You even have your own "toys" in the garage. You offer your kids the kind of life you didn't have, and that, in all respects, is an achievement. But, deep down, you are still not happy with how things are going. You work long hours, and apart from the occasional vacation, you hardly spend time with your family. You are too tired in the evening to play with the kids, and your beautiful house has become a place to sleep and wake up early for work.

This "rat race" is getting to you, and you finally want to find an exit ramp. But at what cost? Are you willing to let go of the luxuries you and your family are already used to, so you can have more time freedom?

Most of us grew up hearing the phrase "money isn't everything." Although this is true to some extent, the phrase became engraved in our subconscious minds that you can't have everything; you often have to sacrifice one for the other. You have to choose between having money and living a miserable life, or being happy and remaining poor. Also, even if you amass so much wealth, it won't be enough to give you everything you'd ever wanted.

You may have not been introduced to the idea that you could have it all. You could still live in the house you wanted, spend time with your family, go on that vacation, and earn enough money to maintain your lifestyle.

So, we work hard every day to ensure we enjoy the small things in life and what we consider luxuries. However, this has come at a cost that more and more people are unwilling to pay. According to researchers, one in every four Americans says they are super stressed while they juggle heavy workloads, manage family and relationships, and try to squeeze in hobbies and personal interests.

That's not all. Research by Gallup reveals that 85% of people hate their jobs, leaving only 15% enjoying and fully engaged in what they do.

Imagine that—on top of a heavy workload, you may not love your job, may dislike your boss and/or coworkers, and there is no such thing as a work-life balance on your horizon.

What is Work-Life Balance?

By definition, work-life balance refers to the state of equilibrium, where you can prioritize your work demands and the demands of your personal life equally. Interestingly, many organizations try to improve work-life balance for their employees, especially now that millennials are taking over the workplace. However, 35% of US full-time workers say that they still struggle immensely with having enough time for their work and personal lives. In fact, it has only gotten worse in the last few years, as it was reported by EY—a firm that provides marketplace insights for companies to interest, inform, and inspire business leaders globally. They reported that the leading causes of dissatisfaction and poor work-life balance are:

- Salaries haven't increased but responsibilities have.
- Increased responsibilities at work, either through understaffed workplaces or promotions.
- Bad bosses.
- Longer work hours.
- Having children.

If these conditions were ideal, people would be happier and more productive at work, and there would be a sprint to get out of bed in the morning instead of pressing the snooze button for the third time. The list provided by EY is not conclusive, and although a lot of people go through these changes, not all have a work-life imbalance. So, how can you find out if your life and work are balanced?

The answer is easy: you need to watch out for signs of work-life imbalance. For instance, you may have added weight because you no longer have time to cook, or perhaps your relationships are suffering. Let's consider the signs in detail, so they are easier to recognize.

Signs of Life-Work Imbalance

1. High-stress levels

A study by The American Institute of Stress found that 40% of participants were highly stressed due to work-related issues, and that stress-related pressure and fear were the leading causes of a work-life imbalance for Americans. Because of heavy workloads, you may find yourself taking a few files back home, so you can work on something urgent or simply catch up on your deadlines.

Eventually, this would become a habit, and you would be leaving the office only to transfer your work to the house where you should be resting and enjoying time with your family. You will also notice that you don't sleep enough hours because you are working late trying to finish up work projects.

2. You are always tired

According to the American Institute of Stress, people highlighted stress as strongly associated with health complications more than financial- and family-related problems. Stress causes physical illnesses and significantly lowers your immune system, making you more prone to fatigue and body ache—anything from headaches, neck pain, and shoulder pain. Sometimes, you may even experience back pain. You will also feel drained and lack the energy to perform your duties and responsibilities, which will lower your performance at work and at home.

Next time you stand up, watch to see if you feel light-headed or like your muscles are sore. You may also be a ticking time bomb, ready to blow up at the slightest disagreement. Mood shifts are also common when you feel low and lack motivation.

3. You are getting out of shape

Gaining weight is a clear sign that you need to move more. However, when you have tons of work waiting for you, it will feel like there's hardly enough time to walk and finish your work. You mostly sacrifice working out and sometimes even cooking a healthy meal by working. With so much to do, take out seems like a good idea, so, the third time this week, pizza and soda will have to do.

As mentioned, your life becomes a cycle—you wake up, drive to work, take work home, sleep, and do it all over again tomorrow. There is hardly time for anything else, and you can't remember the last time you had a walk or played with Skippy, your dog.

4. You are struggling with your relationships

With so little time to do anything but work, your relationships will definitely take a hit. If you don't spend enough time with your partner, kids, and even friends, you could possibly grow apart. When a friend calls to chat, you may tell them you can't talk for long because you are in the middle of answering an urgent email. You even missed your kid's dance recital because your schedule couldn't allow it, or you sold tickets to a concert you've been dying to attend because you had to work last minute.

5. You can't let go of imperfections

There is nothing wrong with aiming for perfection because it ensures you are efficient and productive at work. However, the inability to let go after you've given your best can get in the way of your work-life balance easily. Even when you are striving to do well in your job, it shouldn't be an obsession over every small detail to where it interferes with your personal life. Instead, you should know when something is worth perfecting and when "good" is good enough.

Without a doubt, work-life balance is important. You have to learn to separate your personal and professional life, so they won't interfere with each other. You also can't ignore either of them because balance can help you maintain your mental health. Although not all employees place enough emphasis on mental health at the workplace, studies have shown that work-related stress could lead to stress-related issues, such as anxiety and depression.

The most common issue for many people is burnout, which is when so much pressure and stress is placed on a person that it results in chronic stress. Exhaustion makes people act out of character, whether it's from work overload or feeling unappreciated at work. Maintaining a work-life balance can help you have a positive mental attitude, even when your workload is overflowing. You would also get fulfillment at work and learn to appreciate the efforts you make, thus keeping your mental health in check.

Work-life balance also ensures you maintain productivity at work. Staying for long hours in the office might make you feel like you are contributing or doing something important, but the quality of work could actually be worse. It's better to put forth a laser-focused effort and produce little but sufficient work than spend long hours at work achieving nothing. Studies support the finding that those who maintain a work-life balance are often the most productive people at work.

When your life revolves around work, you will lose many other positive dimensions, some of which make you an attractive and valued employee and person. The interests you have outside work will help you sharpen your skills while making you a rounded and interesting individual. For instance, playing a sport will keep you fit and enable you to develop your focus and problem-solving skills, which are qualities employers look for when hiring.

That's why the hobbies section in your resume is not just "another section," but something to be taken seriously. Besides—you only get one life, and although work is an integral part of it, you can't deny that having fun is what makes life worth living. Spending time with friends and family can help keep you sane and happy while also helping you develop as a person.

When on their deathbeds, people usually cite five major things they regret most about the life they lived—first, they wish they dared to live lives true to themselves and not be sucked into the life that others expected of them. People wished they hadn't worked so much, had the courage to express their feelings without fear, and stayed in touch with their friends. Lastly, people wished they had let themselves be happy.

All these wishes can be achieved by maintaining a proper work-life balance. Although it seems like a pipe-dream, there are a few things you can do to balance your life and work. Here are five to get you started.

1. Break up with perfection

First things first—accept that you cannot be perfect and that even the ideal work-life balance doesn't exist. Hearing about work-life balance is coupled with imaginations of an extremely productive day and leaving early with a smile on your face, knowing that you will get to spend the remainder of the day with friends and family. Although this may happen on occasion, most days will certainly not look like this.

Stop striving for perfect schedules and aim for realistic ones. Some days may mean you focus more on work, whereas others will ask for more time, energy, and interest toward your hobbies, friends, and family. Balance isn't achieved every day, but over time, you will notice that you are balanced. Always ensure you take personal notes on where you are compared to your goals and priorities; that way, you can spare time to attend your kid's football game and travel for work the next day, right after having dinner with your spouse. Remain open-minded and redirect your needs according to priorities. This way, you will find that balance.

2. Find a job you love

Let's look at each day closely. You spend most of the time at home with your family, a little time catching up with friends and personal time, and a chunk of it at work. Granted, most of the time is spent at work and home, sometimes with work taking most of it.

If you are among the unfortunate 85% of Americans who hate their jobs, you are spending half your day at a place you hate and aren't fulfilled. Work is important, but it shouldn't be miserable. If you hate your job, you won't be happy; that's no secret. You will dread getting out of bed in the morning, hate the commute to work, and despise your coworkers.

I don't mean that you have to love every aspect of your job, but you should be content to go to the office, even though you know you will be dealing with something you don't necessarily enjoy. The first sign that you hate your job is when you are unable to find anything enjoyable or worthwhile and find it difficult to do things you love outside work. Instead, you become a toxic person who is always complaining about how terrible your job has been of late. Leaving a work environment you hate, colleagues you don't get along with, and the place you aren't appreciated will be more beneficial in the long term for your mental health and life than sticking around solely for a salary and impressing people you don't like.

3. Unplug

In this tech world, it's hard to be fully unplugged from your devices because that's how you would keep in touch with others. For good or bad, it's how our culture has evolved. However, instead of checking your email during your daily commute, read a novel or check what's happening in the world by reading a newspaper. Transit meditation could also be a great way to get to work. Give yourself time to unplug and worry about emails later instead of leading yourself to potential burnout.

When you get home from work, put your phone on silent and spend an hour cooking for your kids while helping them with homework; or send all calls to voicemail, so you can deal with them later. Eat with your family, go for a jog, or soak in your tub for an hour with a good book and beverage of choice, whatever it takes.

4. Use all your leave days and vacation time

Yes—sometimes unplugging means shutting off work entirely, so you can contemplate current affairs and swim with dolphins. It could even be a one-day stay-cation, in which you spend half the day in bed and the rest of the afternoon swimming laps just because you felt like it. A 2018 study found that 52% of employees reported unused vacation days leftover at the end of the year. No wonder the need for work-life balance is so prevalent!

Most employees fear that taking time off will disrupt their workflow, which will take time to regain. Also, nobody wants to be met with backlog and in-trays overflowing with work that needs their attention when they come back from vacation. This may be true, but the benefits of taking time off far outweigh the downsides. With proper planning, you can take time off and come back to a manageable workload.

5. Take personal time off

Your work, family, and friends are all important, but everyone deserves a little time off to rejuvenate and regain energy. You were an individual before jobs, family, and the worries of this life, so take time to enjoy your hobbies and prioritize what makes you happy just as much as your job. If you aren't intentional with your personal time, you won't find time to do anything outside of work. Take control of your schedule—no matter how hectic it seems—and plan for personal time.

Also, ensure you plan for quality time with your spouse. It's no secret that spending time with them will help build a stronger relationship and improve your quality of life. If your workplace allows it, take the flexible shifts, so you can have more freedom to plan and balance your life.

Work-Life Balance and the Attraction to Network Marketing

The Need for Extra Income

At the heart of work-life balance is the need to have enough income to do the things you truly love. If money wasn't a concern, you would probably love to spend your days traveling, catching up with friends, eating exotic meals, and only working because you wanted to —not because you had to. That's why so many people continue to work in jobs they hate and find it hard to move to doing what they love.

This is one of the selling points for multi-level marketing and an aspect that makes it truly attractive to many people. Compared to 2014, network marketing has been on the rise in terms of the people involved and standard of professionalism in the industry. The integrity of the products and people have all advanced; people are no longer looking at the industry with the proverbial stink eye. In fact, people are becoming more open to opportunities as they seek to balance between earning an income, spending time with family and friends, and traveling the world.

As people get to retirement age, for instance, most are realizing that they aren't as prepared as they would have wanted to be. The retirement fund they saved up won't be enough to last them another 20 or 30 years because life has become more expensive. Nobody predicted that people would live into their eighties and even beyond, which makes living on social security and other government retirement plans insufficient.

People have realized that they can't rely on the government, their kids, or another institution when they get older—the need to amass wealth and be prepared to be self-sufficient when the time comes is being treated with urgency. If you can earn an extra $1,000 a month, you can double your retirement and transform your retirement experience.

You won't have the strength to dig ditches when you are eighty, but you can share a network marketing opportunity with others and earn from it. Does this mean it'll be easy? Certainly not. You will still need to work, brush off a dusty skill set, attend conferences, do follow-ups, among other things to produce the results you desire. However, with a little persistence, the right skills, and a strong network marketing team, you will soon reap the rewards of your labor and have a better chance to retire happy and wealthy.

The Need to Remain Active and Engaged

Spending your days at home doing nothing is exciting for a minute, but the boredom can begin to stress you out. Even after retirement, you will want to remain active and engaged, interacting with others and doing something meaningful with your life. This is as true for people who want to retire as it is for those who want to spend time at home rearing kids. In fact, the need to be active, engaged, and useful is true for all human beings.

That's why stay-at-home moms want to be more than a mother and a wife, usually by building a career and being of service to others. When you are active and engaged, you interact with like-minded people, meeting your need to be social and creating a sense of connection and belonging.

This is the second attraction to the direct sales industry—through conferences, showing products, and building a team, you will get to meet like-minded people and form friendships you would have otherwise never made. You would also learn from each other, grow together, and build each other up in the business. This way, you not only socialize, but you are also of service to others, and you will have a support system that you can rely on.

Work Under Your Own Terms

A survey by PayScale in 2019 found that 69% of working people think flexible work options is the most important factor when evaluating a job prospect. People today want to work, but they want to do it on their own terms and time and earn from their effort. That's why online work opportunities and freelance roles are becoming increasingly more the norm. In fact, America alone boasts about 56.7 million freelancers, according to a report by Freelancers Union. This is an increase of 3.7 million compared to five years ago. Interestingly, 65% of the respondents said they found themselves more productive when they worked in a home office than in a traditional office space, which is no surprise.

And that's not all—a whopping 80% said they would be more loyal to their employer if they were offered flexible working options. Why is this?

From the time you were a toddler, you started learning how to control your life and make decisions for yourself. You learned how to say no, planned your day, and even decided what to wear, eat, and so forth. When you entered the job market, you did receive some form of flexibility, but your hours, schedules, and more were determined by someone else.

When this "power" is given back to you—like it is in direct sales—

you will be bound to becoming more productive. You would decide when to work, how to work, how to achieve the results you desire, and who to interact with in the process. This alone "sets you free" to do the things you love and at your own discretion. Who doesn't want that?

However, the fear that most people have is not getting a paycheck at the end of the month, which is probably why so many people fall out of the direct sales industry. But here's the thing—just because you are working on your own terms doesn't mean you have a one-way ticket to easy money. You still have to use marketing principles, be disciplined, and keep learning. You have to work on devising and testing different strategies, learning from those ahead of you, and waking up every day excited to go to work, even if nobody is pushing you to do it.

Network Marketing offers the possibility that all your hard work will subside once you grow your business. In traditional business models, the more you are promoted, the less time you will have with your family and the more likely you will be to experience work-life imbalance. The MLM business model introduces you to the opposite. The bigger you grow your business, the more time and financial freedom you will have.

People who have achieved this level of success have worked hard for it, so yes, it won't be easy; however, once it's achieved, you will have time to go for vacation, send your kids to a better school, and have enough time to support your team, so they can achieve the same level of success.

CHAPTER SUMMARY

In this chapter, we have touched on why life-work balance is vital for everyone. We learned that:

- 35% of people find it hard to achieve a life-work balance, and 95% of people are not even happy and fulfilled at work.
- High stress-levels, fatigue, gaining weight, and struggling relationships are some signs of work-life imbalance.

- Shunning the unattainable perfectionism, finding a job you love, and unplugging are some ways you can achieve work-life balance.
- Work-life balance does not necessarily mean you would always spend time with your family and are highly productive every day of the week.
- Network marketing is attractive because you can achieve work-life balance easily, since you get to determine your working hours, earn extra income, and socialize with like-minded people.

In chapter six, we will touch on why companies based on a subscription model have exploded and how you can take advantage of it in the direct sales industry.

CHAPTER SEVEN: THE SUBSCRIPTION BUSINESS MODEL EXPLOSION

"What's the best home-based business opportunity in
the world today? Without a doubt, it's network
marketing. Like it or hate it, network marketing
has created more millionaires than any other
industry in history. There's just one problem — it
can be hard if you're not used to it!"

— *KEVIN J. DONALDSON*

CONVENIENCE!

That's what triggers everyone to join a subscription service. A few decades ago, the first job kids had was delivering newspapers to people's doors. It was exciting, and you got to earn a few bucks. Early in the morning, you'd hear little boys and girls riding their bikes and delivering newspapers, or excited teens in their first cars driving around the block, throwing papers to people's doors. As newspapers are about to go extinct—thanks to the internet—these jobs are slowly becoming unavailable.

Also, do you remember hearing clicking sounds at dawn as the milkman passed by? It was a delight. That clicking sound meant that a glass of milk was waiting for you on the breakfast table with a hot plate of cookies. Like the newspapers, however, the milkman seems to have disappeared.

These services have stopped. People prefer to read their paper online and buy their milk at a grocery store. You never see any bottles of milk on the front porch anymore. With the changing customer needs, companies had to look for alternatives or risk extinction. Customers have evolved, in that you and I prefer to engage with a business before buying from them. We seek ownership instead of outcomes, prefer customization instead of generalization, and look out for constant improvement instead of planned obsolescence.

It's no longer business as usual; companies have to work that much harder to get your attention and keep it. That's why there has been an explosion in new types of business models designed to keep you engaged and build long-term relationships.

Building Relationships with Customers Is Vital for Business Success

Building a product or service is a challenging undertaking for many businesses. It's the hardest hurdle any company needs to overcome, but it's not the only factor determining how successful a company will be. As mentioned in chapter four, you and millions of others have more influence in the industry than they did years ago. Today, the focus is not on the product alone. Instead, you want to know more about the product the company is selling, how they are selling it, and what happens once they have sold it. Because this point has already been covered in great detail, I will not repeat it, but I thought it was worth mentioning because of how important relationship building is for businesses.

Also, it's crucial to note that part of creating a long-term relationship has led to the rise of the subscription economy—think Netflix subscription, Amazon Prime, Zendesk Box, Spotify, and even Uber.

Companies are not interested in billing you once when you receive your product, but they want to build a relationship and bill you monthly. On the other hand, you may not have the time, and you are probably not even willing to keep going to the store to buy items that a company could just deliver to your doorstep. Also, think about watching your favorite show on TV, then suddenly being cut off because you hadn't paid for it. Pretty annoying, right?

A subscription, therefore, becomes convenient. You won't have to worry about running out because you know the product or service will be available. You probably won't even think about it and continue using the service—for example, Netflix—as if it were second nature. You only notice the subscription was paid when you see the bill on your credit card statement.

WHY ARE SUBSCRIPTION SERVICES BECOMING SO POPULAR?

Subscription services have helped companies appear as more reliable and consistent income streams. In the past, a company could only bill you once, which meant they had to spend a lot more money on advertising. With a subscription service, the advertisement wouldn't be as aggressive because you are already a customer.

Instead, the company will work harder to earn your loyalty in the beginning and maximize their profits. Let's imagine this scenario: company X has ten subscribers each month. Out of these subscribers, six are consistent, whereas four are not. Company X can only be confident in the six steady customers because they make up most of its revenue. The company can then use this predictable cash flow to make crucial decisions, such as scaling, advertisement budget, and so on.

Measuring the company's financial health and calculating the return on investment becomes easier, since the business no longer has to deal with the unpredictability of one-time sales. A subscription business also gives companies insights that one-time purchases can't provide. These insights can give companies a better understanding of customer behavior and preferences.

By studying this behavior, the company can learn what their customers like, don't mind, and absolutely hate. The insight is then used to influence a wide range of business choices, including making products are fast-moving, how to improve products, product invention, and even how to market them for maximum profit.

The subscription-based business model is also smart from a manu-facturing standpoint. Imagine a company that operates using a consumer-direct or referral marketing business model to market its products. Knowing the vast majority of customers will order each month is cost-effective and allows the company to manufacture just in time. This saves on storage costs and ensures the customers will receive fresh products every time. Since consumers have come to demand higher quality ingredients and don't mind paying for better products, it's a win-win.

According to various studies, the default behavior associated with subscription services is retention. Once you subscribe, you naturally want to continue with the relationship. If a company nails a product or market fit, it can spark customer obsession, which helps them count on subscribers to stick around.

The added simplicity in the subscription business model is also an advantage. With the way the economy is going, vital essentials such as housing, food, and education will continue to rise faster than wages. For a lot of goods, monthly subscription fees are becoming more convenient and cheaper than one-time expenses. They also simplify your life because you can "set and forget." You also retain the power to subscribe and unsubscribe at will.

Personalization is also a significant factor for why subscription services are so popular. Companies that offer such services, such as Stitch Fix, have experienced the level of success they have because of personalized items for every customer. They would ask for the customer's preferences and tailor products according to what the customer loves and appreciates. The customer not only receives cool stuff but also feels seen and appreciated.

Because of how personalized the items are, a customer from that particular fashion and apparel service would be more inclined to stick with them because of the convenience, connection to their preferences, and how they make them feel good, appreciated, and seen. And who doesn't want to feel significant? According to Tony Robbins, the author of *Money Master the Game: 7 Steps to Financial Freedom and Awaken The Giant Within*, significance is one of the most important human needs.

Through personalization, marketers and companies master how to sell products by showing people how significant the item will make them feel. Everyone wants to feel special, which is why personalization helps sell products and services. Personalization speaks to our emotions, making it easier for us to say "yes."

The last thing that makes subscription businesses so successful is curation. Curation is the process of gathering information relevant to a topic, adding value to it, and organizing it in a way that's easy for each individual to understand. Let's use an example to demonstrate—you call a company to ask a question about a service you are thinking of buying. The salesperson is helpful and gives you more details than expected.

At the end of the call, you have all the details about your purchase, benefits you will get, how long it will take to receive your order, and how long before they send you the next one. You probably even know the ingredients used to make the product and the benefit each component offers. This is curation at its best.

The information is gathered and organized in a way that makes you feel like an expert is taking care of your needs and pulling in whatever resources they need to make an exceptional product or service, just for you. Each message you receive feels like it was made for you alone. Think of it as the sprinkled magic behind the suggestions you get on Netflix, the amazing Spotify playlist you discovered, or services like Stitch Fix and Birchbox.

But it's not all rosy. There are a few downsides to note.

DOWNSIDES OF A SUBSCRIPTION BUSINESS

1. Managing churn

Granted, a recurring subscription is one of the main benefits of a company. Month after month, you can charge your customers for products and services and have recurring income. You probably won't even need to advertise to them as much as you did before they joined your subscription service, though that is not always guaranteed.

The customers hold the power to unsubscribe from the service, which means they could cancel at any time. So, although your income is guaranteed to some extent, you may still have to spend more money acquiring more customers and even keeping the current ones on board. Harvard Business School called this the "customer acquisition treadmill," where some are falling off as others get on board. Churning is the biggest challenge that businesses have.

Data from Recury shows that the churning percentage depends on the economy and business industry, but most tend to range from 4.79% to 10.54%. Customers cancel quickly from companies if they feel the service or product is no longer superior.

2. Stiff competition

A Fetch survey conducted in 2019 found that 75% of people find it hard to choose a subscription service because there are just too many on the market. 40% of respondents also said they planned on reducing the number of subscriptions they had. Let's consider Netflix, for example, the company known to have started the extinction of DVDs and cable.

When they started, they were largely unchallenged and had the largest market share with millions of homes subscribing to the service. Hulu, their main competition at the time, was at a distant second. However, recently, major media brands and networks have joined the bandwagon and wanted a piece of the pie. Disney, Facebook, NBC, Apple, and Amazon Prime are giving Netflix a run for their money. It's no longer business as usual because the same market share Netflix dominated is now shared between major brands.

The explosion of subscription services has increased the choices you have in industries and segments. Having too many choices has, however, led to subscription fatigue. This refers to customers getting tired of subscribing to services because there are too many businesses in that niche. For instance, you may have to pay for AMC, Netflix, and Hulu because one service provider doesn't have all your favorite shows.

Some industry experts are beginning to give warning signs of subscription fatigue, saying that consumers simply don't have enough money to go round. Obviously, consumers will start to drop one service in favor of another or simply go without some of them entirely. In fact, some research suggests that at least one million Netflix subscribers canceled following the launch of Disney's streaming service, Disney+.

3. Balancing profitability and accessibility

To run a successful subscription service, companies must charge enough money to cover finance charges, depreciation, and other operational costs. These costs can push monthly pricing above what consumers consider a "good deal." The business must also offer value, build trust, and a strong relationship with the buyer, which costs money. Some companies find it hard to add value, run the business, and remain profitable at the same time. Remember—subscribing is just as easy as unsubscribing.

According to MoonClerk, this imbalance is brought by the loss of interest in the service. You may have looked at your cable bills and wondered why you pay for it when you don't watch any of the channels. The company must continuously think of how they will keep you interested, so you don't get bored and unsubscribe. That's why companies like Birchbox and FabFitFun keep their customers excited by including new products every month. This interest helps ensure they have enough to cover their costs, advertise, create new products, and remain profitable.

How Subscription SErvices Can Propel your MLM Business

1. Cuts across all industries

Just to recap, multi-level marketing companies pay representatives because of two major activities—the first is through selling products and services that the company offers, whereas the other is through commissions earned once a downline sells a product or service. I have mentioned that you can earn from selling products and from recruiting a team, downline, or organization.

For most direct sales/multi-level marketing companies, you have to buy a certain amount of products each month. This monthly purchase in itself is a subscription service. Some companies have set the investment at $100 or more. So, how can you recover this money and even make a profit from sales?

Let's go back to our previous example of beauty products. When your friend notices how great you looked with that foundation, or how your fine lines have faded, you obviously referred her to your company's products. After using the product for herself for a month, she realized what a gem she has fallen into and now wants to know she can get it every month.

You talk to her about joining the company and becoming a distributor herself, but she isn't interested, even though she loves the products. So, don't nag her about joining the company. Instead, sell her the products she loves, since you will get a commission from them.

Like other companies in this space, you will also be benefiting through the "subscription" your friend makes by purchasing products from you every month.

This concept doesn't apply to the beauty product alone.

Let's consider the health and fitness industry—without a doubt, the food you eat has some nutrients to help you maintain good health. These nutrients include calcium, vitamins, and magnesium. Millions of people aren't getting enough nutrients from their diet. This is according to Harvard Health Publishing.

It's a fact that the "normal" American meal is packed with nutrient-poor processed food from refined grains and added artificial sugars. People have meals with a soda or wine, ignoring water and herbal teas. White bread is favored over whole-grain bread when making sandwiches, and when people don't feel like cooking, many would rather eat pizza or french fries rather than mix a healthy salad. These foods lead to inflammation and the chronic diseases we discussed in chapter two.

Harvard Health Publishing noted that, even when you eat a healthy, well-balanced diet, you may still fall short of all the nutrients the body needs. It's a consequence of the depleted soil we grow our plants in and natural causes such as aging. As you grow older, for example, energy needs change, and you tend to eat less than you did when you were young, active, and vibrant. Obviously, the food you eat won't provide 100% of the nutrients your body needs to function the way nature intended.

Supplements become your second best option to ensure these nutrients are delivered to your body, keeping it working at optimum levels. Anyone in this industry will therefore benefit from selling supplements as a recurring subscription to customers.

This applies to consumer goods as well; think of cleaning products, disinfectants, snack foods, coffee, and essential oils as much as you do beauty products and diet supplements. The sale of products increases your potential for recurring income, to the extent that the income you earn from your customers can be used for your own purchases from the company. Thus, now you're saving money on these purchases and enjoying an additional income stream.

REDUCING THE IMPACT ON THE ENVIRONMENT

Today, people are more conscious of the impact harmful chemicals have on them, their kids, and pets. Thus, they prefer to work with companies that care for the environment, especially if the products are affordable. Representatives can take advantage of this because some of the products found in the consumer direct and network marketing industry consist of more natural ingredients that don't harm the earth. Some companies even offer concentrated formulas that make several bottles once mixed with water from your own tap, making the packaging and shipping even more eco friendly, and the price point more affordable to consumers.

This includes everyday consumable products. For instance, pet shampoo, body wash, disinfectants, and essential oils. It could even be beauty products such as perfume and foundation.

Some companies extract the components they need for production through natural means, which further cares for the environment. They also urge customers to help the company recycle whenever possible. However, it's not just the environment that needs saving.

Since the products are organic, they are also safer for you compared to their counterparts. So, just because a product is natural does not mean you have to compromise your beauty regimen. Products packed with toxins and chemicals are absorbed into the skin and cause more damage than good. If they work, it's only for a while because the toxins eventually harm you.

1. You can build relationships and deliver value

Earlier on, we said that people don't buy products; they make buying decisions based on emotions. For instance, if you have fine lines under your eyes, you probably won't feel as confident as if you didn't have them. On another note, perhaps you have a potbelly that restricts you from wearing certain clothes.

When buying a health supplement or slimming tea, you will most likely be buying that feeling you anticipate when you finally get to the size you want or when your fine line disappears. Now, let's assume you are a distributor and want to sell a product to a friend or colleague. You just joined a company that sells weight loss products, and you have lost a couple of pounds yourself. Your confidence has soared, and you are looking better than you have in years.

Let's look at a scenario—your friend, Bruce from accounting, has expressed his desire to shed a few pounds. He doesn't feel as confident because of his weight, and he has mentioned it to you a couple times. As you have lunch, he repeats it as he compliments you on your great success.

At this point, it's natural to tell him that he can get the same results and show him how you did it. However, you have to remember where he is right now emotionally if you are to package your product right. You have to sell this emotion so well that Bruce starts to believe that it's possible for him. If he doesn't believe it, he won't buy it.

I've been in the MLM space for decades, and one of the most important things I learned as a newbie is to be authentic when talking about the products. Companies don't tell you to do this because it could look like a hoax—it shows the prospect that the products are great, and they can achieve the same result that you did. Think about it—when you discovered how buying cleaning products could be seamless, you were naturally excited to talk to your friends about it. The same concept applies here.

According to Brian Tracy, author of *The Psychology of Selling*, value is the difference between your price and the benefits your customer perceives they will get. If your customer believes that the benefit is worth the price, they will, without a doubt, buy from you. It makes sense to teach people the value they will get, how your product or service will help them, and how much your products or service will help them solve their problem and achieve their goal. In fact, the more focus you place on the value, the less important the price becomes.

The next time you meet a prospect, forget about the price and focus on showing them the value and prospect of how the products will help them and the feeling they will get from obtaining the product.

Chapter Summary

In this chapter, we covered a number of things, mainly about the importance of building relationships with customers. The following is what we talked about:

- 89% of customers have higher expectations for customer service now.
- Companies have to be careful about how they engage with customers if they want to improve their customer experience.
- Building relationships with customers can help a company retain the customer, build brand loyalty, and increase customer satisfaction.
- Subscription services have grown in popularity because of the convenience they offer to customers.
- Companies that can build relationships with their clients have more subscribers, and thus higher sales and retention.

- MLM representatives can cultivate emotional relationships with others to sell products and recruit downlines, teams, and organizations.

In the next chapter, you will learn strategies that you can use to find the right network marketing, consumer direct, direct sales, or MLM company.

CHAPTER EIGHT: FINDING THE RIGHT FIT

"…network marketing is a dynamic, exciting, and rapidly expanding profession worldwide. It's also a legitimate profession (though some will try to convince you otherwise) that generates wealth for millions of individuals and contributes positively to our global society."

— ZIG ZIGLAR & JOHN HAYES, *NETWORK MARKETING FOR DUMMIES*

IMAGINE YOU ARE AT WORK OR BROWSING THE INTERNET WHEN someone you haven't spoken to in a long time hits you up. They want to meet you for coffee and catch up, or maybe they invite you for dinner at their place. When you finally meet them, they tell you about this exciting opportunity and show you a presentation on a DVD. That's when it hits you—you have walked into another network marketing, direct sales, or MLM presentation. When the presentation is over, you promise to think about it, then go ahead and block said friend everywhere, so they won't bother you again.

Or, perhaps you consider the idea, but you are still skeptical of joining because of the past horror stories or negative press you have heard about the industry. As you think of what to do, however, your friend continues to contact you about deciding when to join. Either you become appalled and take this as a red flag and keep a tight grip on your money, give the products a try, or make the decision to join the company.

Let's assume you join. You attend another meeting, and you are told to use the same strategy your team leader or upline used. You try it out but only get a handful of people in your organization or team and don't earn enough money to sustain your bills or even buy groceries. Dejected, you quit and vow never to join another direct sales company, network marketing, or MLM.

Sadly, this is the introduction many people have had with direct sales companies, and although it's not entirely false, it gives off all the wrong signals. It's also the opposite of the strategies we have covered so far.

But, is that it? Is it impossible to choose a company?

No, it's not. However, the answer is a little more complex than that. First, let's consider a few things that you must keep in mind before choosing a network marketing company.

Understand How Direct Sales, Network Marketing, and MLMs Market Themselves

If you have ever attended a meeting or presentation, you probably know the drill; you may be in a room full of people, and someone, perhaps a team leader or upline, will start by welcoming you and giving you a brief introduction as to why you are there. Next, they will use a DVD provided by the company to show you the opportunity and possibilities you will have by joining.

Social Media has also allowed those who are actively pursuing a consumer direct, or mlm business the ability to effectively reach into nearly every corner of the world with their product and message.

However, I think everyone needs to remember that not everything that glitters is gold, and it's naïve to assume that it is. You shouldn't let the hype be the only reason you join a company in the same way you shouldn't buy a product just because you saw an ad on TV. There is way more to consider when choosing a company than basing your decisions on an advertisement. You shouldn't necessarily trust every ad you see on TV or social media, so why should you trust a company because you saw a DVD? Instead, take your time to research the company and learn more about its products, services, mission, vision, and goals before joining.

The truth is, you don't have to be among the first people to join a company because that's irrelevant to how much money you will earn. Therefore, take your time to consider all factors.

THE PEOPLE

Remember that friend who asked you to come for coffee? In some cases, this is the first person who will show you the business and path to follow. Think of them as a customer representative of the company —the experience you get from them will largely determine if you will succeed or fail. Trust can't be given; it has to be earned, and although you work with your upline, team leader, or sponsor, you will know if they are to be trusted or not.

It helps if the person has previous industry experience because if they are new at it like you, you will be in the same rocky boat. That doesn't mean a newbie can't recruit you, though. Remember—even your newbie friend has an upline or team leader who will likely have more experience. Find out how accessible they are in terms of answering questions and helping you clarify what you don't understand.

Also, you will be spending a lot of time with that person, so you must get along and like them. Unlike in a job where you have to put up with your boss, consumer direct and network marketing companies don't operate that way. Liking your colleagues means you will have a good working relationship, especially if you can feel your efforts are appreciated.

I have to warn you, though; just because you found a great sponsor or team leader does not mean they will do the work for you. You still have to get off your butt and work your way to the top.

When you attend a meeting, look around at the kind of people the business attracts. Check if they are the kind of people you like to be associated with. You may be attending company training and events together, and interacting with them will be crucial for your success. It helps when you work with people you like.

In addition to liking them—or at least feeling confident that you can be with them in the long term—you need to be aware of the tools. Is there a well-laid out roadmap or system that you can pick up and run with to achieve some level of success? If the person who is looking to sponsor you is flying by the seat of their pants and throwing mud against the proverbial wall just to see what sticks, chances are that's what you'll be doing as well. Your sponsor doesn't necessarily need to have their own system, but they should at least have access to tools that have been proven in the marketplace and be willing to spend the time training you to use those tools and acquire the skills you'll need.

Also, consider this—just because your friend or acquaintance has found their niche or company home doesn't mean it's the right fit for you. If you do not have a genuine interest in marketing the products, service, and/or opportunity, keep looking. You may desire to be a customer only, and that's fine. It's better to know in the beginning than to be frustrated all the time and unable to accomplish any measure of success.

One last thought on sponsors (team leader, enrollee, support team): is everyone welcome, or are they just looking for their next superstar? In other words, if you choose to be a customer only or build the business part-time, are they equally dedicated to helping you reach the goals you've chosen for yourself, or will they be pushing to re-create you in their own image?

CHECK THE COMPANY PROFILE

The US Small Business Administration Office Of Advocacy has some interesting facts about companies. According to their research, 20% of new businesses fail within the first years of inception, whereas 45% fail within the first five years. By year ten, only 33% survive. This is why company longevity tops my list as the first thing you should have in mind when researching a company.

Although not all companies will fail within the first two years, it is my personal opinion to stay clear of consumer direct, network marketing, MLM, and direct sales companies that are five years or fewer years old. Remember that just because you got in early does not automatically mean you will make money; that shouldn't be a factor.

It will be disheartening for you and your team if, after building for years, the company goes under with all your money and investments. This is common with young companies because they may not necessarily have enough capital to run and sustain themselves. Check if the company has been in the market for a while (at least five years) and whether they are financially stable. With such a company, your group-building efforts won't go to waste.

Tons of network marketing companies have come and gone over the years because of legal issues (some are illegal). Also, like traditional companies, the owner is unable to keep the business running. Strong leadership is second on my list. It is vital to look at the experience that the founders and management team have. Who are they and what's their mission? Do they have integrity? Can you find their past experience easily?

If top management is known to start scams and disappear with people's money, avoid that company, even when the opportunity sounds too good to pass up. It's better to be safe than work hard and not get paid. As for legal issues, you can easily learn if that company has a bunch of lawsuits via a quick Google search. The Better Business Bureau and the Federal Trade Commission are great places to check. These two organizations have access to thousands of lawsuits against companies. Also, check social media forums and see what others are saying about the company.

Most people on social media are surprisingly honest and will give their opinion if something negative happened to them when working with a company. Be discerning, however—just because something negative gets posted on social media, does not mean it's true. There are trolls who post incorrect information for reasons solely their own;

maybe their ex is at that company, or they used to be and decided to go somewhere else. Just because it's online does not mean it's the truth.

If the company has court cases, it will be hard to keep the news off platforms, even if the company spends time trying to bury the truth. So, get your reading glasses on and conduct your own due diligence. The Direct Selling Association is a great resource for this and can be found at http://www.dsa.org.

Does the company have clear and easily accessible policies, guidelines, and rules of conduct that are applied evenly across the entire company? If they run more of a good ole boy network instead of a company where each person is treated fairly and equally, look somewhere else.

The Products

The product line rounds out the top three most important factors to consider when researching a company to join. Here are some questions to ask yourself—are the products of superior quality to those widely available on the market? Are they safer, unique, or protected by trade secrets, proprietary formulas, and patents? Are they products that aren't easily accessible at a regular store and can only be obtained through that company? Does INDEPENDENT Research verify them? Are products only purchased for a short season in someone's life? Are they consumable staples that create customers who love the brand and buy regularly? Remember that monthly consumption generates ongoing, residual income. Are they competitively priced, or will buying them break what may be a carefully planned family budget? Is it a smart economic choice that provides excellent value to the customer? Where are the products manufactured? How reliable are supply chains and ingredients? Are they recession proof—meaning, products that people purchase in good and bad economies? What is the reorder rate?

Low attrition is fourth. Does the company provide education, training, and up-to-date resources? If you notice the company you want to join doesn't offer an avenue for training, you can be sure you won't have the right tools to succeed. MLM, direct sales, and network marketing companies that succeed don't spend all their time training you to be a recruiter; instead, they help you become a business leader. Training and conferences are more than spending two hours listening to a sales pitch and watching a DVD while looking at a brochure; it involves understanding business concepts that will help you market the products and personal development classes that help you become successful. You will also learn networking, planning, communication, and goal-setting, which are vital to success in the industry.

You may also want to look for a company with a global presence. You may not have plans of going global today, but perhaps, in a few years, you will want to live a digital, nomad lifestyle, affording your kids a chance to live or study abroad. Knowing you can spread your wings to other countries becomes a significant advantage.

Most MLM, direct sales, and network marketing companies are very keen on the products they send out to the market, but it also helps first to find out if the companies are true to their word. If they say their products are organic, what ingredients are they using? Are they sourcing the ingredients with integrity? How do they dispose of waste after production?

You may have to research to find this kind of information, but it will be worth your while. Also, the products from a company have to offer tremendous value to the marketplace, be affordable, and generally a money-back guarantee. If the price point is too high, you will have a problem selling products when people cannot afford them.

In my opinion, network marketing, consumer direct, and the direct sales industry is about creating long-lasting income—not a one-time sale or commission. This is where marketplace demand comes into play. For instance, selling a unique product that nobody has ever heard of could mean lower demand, even when it has little to no competition.

You will probably never see products from direct sales and MLM in a store. Consumers must have a great reason to consider your products and buy from your company. It's not just about the money, but about the value they will receive when they purchase the products. It's important to sell a product that offers value, not only to you, but to a lot of people.

If the product doesn't have real-world value, you may be looking at a pyramid scheme, so beware. Start by purchasing the product. If you are happy with the results you get, then you probably have a winner. When you are excited about a product, you will automatically want to share it with others. It was the same with that friend of mine who told me about cleaning products that I had no interest in purchasing. If she wasn't excited about it, she would not have mentioned it.

Although earning money is great, it should never be the only focus. Sure, you are looking for a legitimate company because you want to make money, but when money is your only driving force, you are setting yourself up to fail. You have to like what you are selling, the people you are working with, and the company.

Ultimately, your success is directly proportionate to your effort. You have to get off your couch and introduce products while prospecting and building your team. Listen to your team leaders and follow in their footsteps. Success leaves clues, and if you follow them, you will succeed. Thus, don't try to reinvent the wheel; learn and use what works.

COMPENSATION PLAN

The compensation or payment plan basically explains how you will be paid. Where your money is concerned, you should pay close attention. Each company will have a different compensation plan, and it's important that you understand it. If it's too complicated or up to someone other than you—meaning shifting "legs" or teams around for you to collect a check—that is a red flag.

There are four main types of plans common to the industry: The Binary, The Universal, The Stair Step Breakaway, and The Matrix.

All compensation plans work for some, but you must spend time understanding the one the company you are considering uses. Learn it well enough to explain it to others and answer all their questions adequately. If the compensation plan is too complicated and you cannot understand and see how you would be able to derive an income, let alone explain it to others, run. Complicated payment plans often mean that a company has a lot to hide, making it harder for you to get paid. And, if you can't get paid, you may be dealing with a get-rich-quick scheme. People who have fallen into this trap end up devastated when they realize they aren't getting paid for all their hard work.

Know what you will have to produce each month to collect any commissions or royalties before you invest any time or money. I advocate for a model based on a low personal production requirement. I have experience with both, and let me assure you, it's much more fun and lucrative knowing what I purchase is for my own use and not contingent on receiving my check. I'm not ordering inventory just to qualify for a check.

It's also wise to ask for company-published statistics on what their rep's earn. Some companies may have this on their company site or available upon request.

As we've discussed, income is earned by introducing customers to the product line and sponsoring or enrolling others in your team. Although it's not the only factor to consider, it's usually advantageous when you can sponsor as many people as possible. The difference a couple of people make can be enormous for your income. Let's assume you start by sponsoring four people. Your network, team, or downline, will have 4, 16, 64, 256, 1024, 4096, then 16384 up to level six. If you sponsor four more people to have a total of eight, your team will look like this by level six: 8, 64, 512, 2048, 16384, 35356, 524288.

A difference of four people has made such a massive impact on your earnings, which is why having a cap on how many people you can sponsor is not such a good idea. Also, people will drop off along the way. So, if you have a large team/organization, you will have an income when attrition takes place.

When researching a company, note how many people you need to sponsor to earn a decent living. If you need to get to level six to make enough money to live on, be wary. A great company compensates you for a couple of people as much as they do hundreds of sign-ups. Obviously, the more people you sponsor, the more products you move, and the higher your income.

Another thing to note where compensation plans are concerned is that commissions are made on the sale of products and not membership or enrollment fees. As we mentioned before, this is a big difference between legitimate MLM companies and pyramid schemes.

Membership fees cannot sustain a company and will inevitably lead to the company's crumbling with thousands of people unpaid.

First, ask whether you can make money if your network prefers to consume the product and not recruit anybody. The answer should be a resounding YES—and if it's not, be wary.

Remember that some companies require that you buy a certain number of products each month. Sometimes, the monthly expense will prove to be too high, and you may prefer to discontinue. This means it's vital that you read the fineprint, so you know if the company has a return policy that you can take advantage of. A company that enables you to recoup your investment is considered a low-risk company, and it's usually the best organization to join. This way, you are sure you won't lose all your investment if you change your mind.

YOURSELF

The last thing I plan to touch on is the person sitting in your chair —*YOU*. The industry is a profession like any other. What do I mean? Some people are meant to be teachers, landscapers, IT, administrators, or truck drivers, so examine yourself carefully before you hop in. Can everyone become a part of a network marketing, consumer direct, MLM or direct sales company? Yes. Should everyone? No. Although nearly everyone can benefit from the products that I have experience with, not all should pursue the business aspect. Some are better suited to buy and use the products, which is completely fine.

After you've completed your due diligence and chosen a company, examine yourself. Take an honest inventory of your skills and look into your past to see where you've been successful (a job or project) that you can build upon. What skills or training do you need and where can you get them? Do you already have a background that is a perfect fit within the industry, or will you need to learn a different skill set? Had you joined the industry before and quit? What is different this time around? Self-examination can help you determine if this is the best career move for you.

One of the benefits you may be surprised at is how you grow as a person. Few industries force you to examine yourself and address your motivations, agenda, and why you think the way you do. The direct sales, MLM, and consumer direct industry teaches you leadership and entrepreneurship and how to duplicate yourself in others with the same goals—not how to be someone else's employee.

You are forced to think about your legacy. It's way more than "firing your boss" or "living the laptop lifestyle;" it is about crafting a complete life for yourself. This is not just in terms of lifestyle or money that gets passed down to future generations (though that would be awesome), but who you become as a person in terms of transferable marketable skills, leadership, philanthropy, and working with great people who may become your lifelong friends.

I have had the pleasure of meeting some of the most generous human beings who truly inspire others. Many of those who have "made it" to the top in the industry have donated large sums of money to revitalize their hometowns, build museums, sponsor orphanages, pay anonymously for medical bills, and selflessly mentor an up-and-coming generation. Things that matter and make an impact on this world long term—people.

Chapter Summary

In this chapter, we have looked at an in-depth analysis of what you need to check when looking for a company to join. We looked at the following:

- Joining a company early doesn't mean you will earn the most money.
- Make sure the company has a great business community that's willing and ready to support you through the business. It's important to have a good relationship with your sponsor/upline/support team.
- Understand the compensation plan well enough that you can explain it to others and know how you will be paid. You should earn from both recruitment and product sales.
- When you are excited about a product, talking about it

with others will be easy and second nature. Products should have market demand and a great price point and offer value to customers.

- A good company invests in training and recognizes that product sales and recruiting are essential to your success.
- Your success will largely depend on your effort. You can join the best company and not succeed if you are a couch potato. Put in the effort required and you will win.

FINAL WORDS

If you were to start a business, you would have to get a business permit, rent an office, fit it with equipment, and hire staff. This is without factoring in marketing, advertising, and product creation, securing supply chains, logistics, among other expenses. Network marketing/direct sales/MLM gives you an opportunity to start a business at low cost. The industry features a low upfront investment to purchase your first product kit, which you may elect to introduce to your friends, family, and contacts. Or you may elect to deploy technology & automation instead.

According to a study by AARP, at least one in thirteen Americans have participated in an MLM/direct sales company at some point. This means that some people you will be introducing your company to will have prior experience. Luckily, the industry has come of age and is spreading far and wide thanks to the internet. However, even with tech, you still need to roll up your sleeves, show up, and work. On paper, the concept always seems easy. With having bought the products and introducing them to others, your goal is to have yur team or organization multiply as if by magic, but it requires work!

Sometimes, family and friends will be the last people to support your efforts. This is sad but true.

The shift in customer behavior has also changed how businesses operate. The power is in the hands of the consumer. Successful companies study their customers' behavior and change with the times, offering clients products and services that meet their needs. The company also knows it's important to meet the customers halfway by being present on social media platforms and the internet. Being online means they can answer all questions promptly, take care of a customer's short-term concerns, and learn about their long-term needs.

As a network marketing/direct sales representative, you need to understand how your customers' needs are changing. Do they prefer subscriptions to your products, or are they comfortable with one-time purchases? Do they prefer to connect on social media or meet you for coffee? Knowing this can help you build lasting relationships for a successful MLM/consumer direct business.

You have heard of people who have little to no education become self-made millionaires through the industry, whereas a university professor didn't make a dime. While there are no doubt many possible reasons, the difference could be that they knew how to create a marketing system, enabling them to expose a lot of people to their products while catering to their needs, whereas another person didn't.

People from all walks of life are welcome to join the industry. There is a low barrier to enter that welcomes anyone who genuinely believes in the company's mission and vision. Once you pick what success means to you, get to work and never look back, no matter the challenges you face. Maybe you have a modest goal to cover your cell phone bills, or it's important to you to have a nice family vacation each year, life-changing income, or create a legacy to be passed down to future generations.

Whatever your goal is, remember to start with a single step and always be willing and ready to learn, so you can keep moving forward. Use the skills you are taught—some of which you will never learn in a class setting—to propel your company to success and profitability.

Remember that success is not a mistake; it's a series of decisions, strategies, and skills.

Thanks for taking this journey with me. I hope you have been enlightened and even a little entertained, and that you may have more insight into the changes in consumer behavior and how it is affecting the direct sales industry as a whole. There's good and bad in everything, so if you are considering direct sales, consumer direct, network marketing, or MLM business, take the time to do your research to find the best fit for you. I've included a couple of worksheets on the following pages to help you do just that. If you follow through with these two exercises, you will improve your odds of finding the company that is right for you and dramatically increase your chances of realizing your goals.

After many years in this industry, I don't claim to be a guru or master at anything. My desire for you is to pursue the path and goals that are right for you. We only get one chance on this planet, so live life intentionally, with purpose, and with passion.

All the best,

WORKSHEET 1

PICKING THE RIGHT COMPANY FOR YOU

	Company Name	Company Name	Company Name	Company Name
	Website Annual Sales	Website Annual Sales	Website Annual Sales	Website Annual Sales
Compensation Plan	Model	Model	Model	Model
Taxes	1099? Yes ___ No ___	1099? Yes ___ No ___	1099? Yes ___ No ___	1099? Yes ___ No ___
Leadership Who's at the helm?				
Products	Industry? Market Demand? Affordable Price Point? $ Back Guarantee? Unique?	Industry? Market Demand? Affordable Price Point? $ Back Guarantee? Unique?	Industry? Market Demand? Affordable Price Point? $ Back Guarantee? Unique?	Industry? Market Demand? Affordable Price Point? $ Back Guarantee? Unique?
Training	Online, Webinars, Dvd?	Online, Webinars, Dvd?	Online, Webinars, Dvd?	Online, Webinars, Dvd?
Marketing Tools				

Prospective Company Evaluation

Based on the tables above, do I have enough information to narrow my choice down to 3 companies? Yes:_____ No:_____

List my top 3 choices and why they make the cut:

1. Company Name: _____

Why I chose them:

_____

_____

_____

_____

_____

_____

_____

Questions for prospective mentor/enroller/coach. Repeat these for your top 3 finals.

Prospective Mentor Name: _____

Phone: _____

Email: _____

1. Investment. How much to get started?_____

Are there different levels/options? How does that affect my earnings?

_____

_____

_____

_____

_____

_____

_____

3. Do I have to store inventory? _____

4. Do I have to collect any money for orders, ship or deliver?

_____

5. What kind of training or events does the company offer?

_____

_____

_____

_____

_____

_____

_____

6. Do you provide training for your team/organization: _____

Training site? Cost?

_____

Webinar? Cost?

_____

Other tools? Cost?

_____

7. What income level are you at? You may ask this if you choose, but keep in mind, everyone's income is their own business. In my personal opinion, I believe this is in poor taste. You may feel entitled or it is important for you to know how much they are making, and chances are your prospective mentor/coach is used to getting this question, but if they choose not to answer, or speak in generalities with regard to their income you need to respect their wish for some level of privacy. They don't know you, or your intentions. In my experience, being among the top income earners in a particular company does not make them a good mentor or coach, just as being new to a company, or not among the top income earners does not make them a bad one. The important take-away is, are they willing and able to help you succeed?

_____

_____

_____

_____

_____

_____

_____

8.   Other:

_____

_____

_____

_____

_____

_____

_____

2. Company Name:

_____

Why I chose them:

_____

_____

_____

_____

_____

_____

_____

Prospective Mentor Name: _____

Phone: _____

Email: _____

1. Investment. How much to get started?_____

2. Are there different levels/options? How does that affect my earnings?

_____

_____

_____

_____

_____

_____

_____

3. Do I have to store inventory?

_____

4. Do I have to collect any money for orders, ship or deliver?

_____

5. What kind of training or events does the company offer?

_____

_____

_____

_____

_____

_____

_____

6. Do you provide training for your team/organization:

_____

Training site? Cost?

_____

Webinar? Cost?

_____

Other tools? Cost?

_____

7. What income level are you at?

_____

8. Other:

_____

_____

_____

_____

_____

_____

_____

3. Company Name: _____

Why I chose them:

_____

_____

_____

_____

_____

_____

_____

Prospective Mentor Name: _____

Phone: _____

Email: _____

1. Investment. How much to get started?_____

2. Are there different levels/options? How does that affect my earnings?

_____

_____

_____

_____

_____

_____

_____

3. Do I have to store inventory?

_____

4. Do I have to collect any money for orders, ship or deliver?

_____

5. What kind of training or events does the company offer?

_____

_____

_____

_____

_____

_____

_____

6. Do you provide training for your team/organization:

_____

Training site? Cost?

_____

Webinar? Cost?

_____

Other tools? Cost?

_____

7. What income level are you at?

_____

8. Other:

_____

_____

_____

_____

_____

_____

_____

WORKSHEET 2

KNOW YOURSELF

Take a few moments and really think before you answer each item listed below.

1. Personal Mission Statement:

You will be light years ahead if you develop your own personal mission statement before you pick a company, set an income goal, or begin planning your dream home. Really spend some time and effort on this. It should be the standard you measure everything else against. Working this out in the beginning may keep you from choosing the wrong path, saving you tons of time, energy and effort. It's also a great beginning point for knowing your values and motives. Write down 1-2 sentences for each role in your life (spouse, parent, entrepreneur, ect.)

Spouse:

_____

_____

_____

_____

_____

_____

_____

Parent:

_____

_____

_____

_____

_____

_____

Entrepreneur:

_____

_____

_____

_____

_____

_____

Other (Job, Volunteer, Elder Care):

_____

_____

_____

_____

_____

_____

_____

2. Income goal:

_____

Don't call it good when you can write down an amount per month or per year that you would like to make. What's the underlying meaning behind the amount? What would a certain income each month allow you to do? What does it represent? The answer should evoke a strong emotional response, if it doesn't, you're not digging deep enough.

_____

_____

_____

_____

_____

_____

_____

Why is this so important to me?

_____

_____

_____

_____

_____

_____

_____

Time:

How much time do you have per week right now? Be realistic.

_____

Is my time congruent with my income goals? _____

If not, what needs to change? My income goals, or time commitment?

_____

If you will be building your business around your current job, what days/hours will you be realistically able to carve out?

_____

_____

_____

_____

_____

_____

_____

Are there activities you may need to stop doing in order to make time for your business?

_____

_____

_____

_____

_____

_____

_____

If you need to end certain activities or current commitments list them here and an end date for each.

_____

_____

_____

_____

_____

_____

_____

Given my current choice, and knowing what I know right now, do I possess the skills required to get started?

_____

If you answered yes, list them here:

_____

_____

_____

_____

_____

_____

_____

If not, list the skills you need to acquire and how you can learn the skills you need (mentor, webinar, online course, etc.)

_____

_____

_____

_____

_____

_____

_____

Is my spouse on board? _____

If not, you need to have an in-depth and honest conversation.

Tip: If your spouse is hesitant, or gun shy because you may have tried things in the past that didn't work out, you can demonstrate your commitment by completing these worksheets and presenting them with well thought out answers before you have a conversation.

List topics and any concerns you each have here:

_____

_____

_____

_____

_____

_____

_____

Resolutions to concerns listed above:

_____

_____

_____

_____

_____

_____

_____

If your spouse will maintain their job/career, will they need to take on additional hours to compensate for any income gaps?

_____

_____

_____

_____

_____

_____

_____

If so, given your current income needs, how much additional income will need to be made?

_____

If you have very young (preschool age) children, who is responsible for their care?

_____

Why do I want this? Income, status, lifestyle, time freedom, or personal achievement?

_____

_____

_____

_____

_____

_____

Mid-way Check: Now that you have made it this far evaluate your answers to this point. Is this goal in harmony with my vision, beliefs and values? If yes, GREAT- keep going. If not write down what doesn't line up and address those points.

_____

_____

_____

_____

_____

_____

Lifestyle: A lifestyle is more than income. It's a whole and complete life.
Write down what a typical day looks like when you have reached your goal.

_____

_____

_____

_____

_____

_____

_____

Where do you live?
_____

Do you work with your spouse, or do they maintain their own career or
business?

_____

_____

_____

_____

_____

_____

_____

If you have children where do they go to school? Private, homeschool, public?

_____

_____

_____

_____

_____

_____

_____

Where do you vacation?

_____

_____

_____

_____

_____

_____

_____

Investments?

_____

_____

_____

_____

_____

_____

_____

Philanthropy?

_____

_____

_____

_____

_____

_____

_____

Do I want to leave a legacy for my children (future children)?

_____

_____

_____

_____

_____

_____

_____

How do I define Legacy?

_____

_____

_____

_____

_____

_____

_____

For additional resources, newsletters and occasional freebies go to cdwolfebooks.com or networkmarketingreboot.com and sign up for our email list.

How To Build An Empire In Any Economy: 101 Business Growth Tips You Need Now

https://www.amazon.com/dp/B088NKTM88

For additional resources, newsletters and occasional freebies go to cdwolfebooks.com or networkmarketingreboot.com and sign up for our email list.

AUTHOR'S NOTE

Thank you for reading my book! This is my first and it took me a long time to muster the courage to stick my head up above the crowd. Can you relate? I have 25 years experience in this industry and remember what it was like in the beginning. So many questions—who, what, where, when, and how? Many who are exploring this industry simply join the first company they come across without knowing more than the company's name and a brief synopsis of the products and/or services they offer. You wouldn't look for a career or a spouse that way, would you? Hopefully not! This has unfortunately led to many people having a less-than-pleasant experience and is one of the biggest reasons I wanted to write this, if nothing else than to spark a conversation or help someone learn how to explore further.

Now that you've finished this book, I would truly appreciate it if you would take a moment to share your thoughts by leaving a review. I look forward to reading it and wish you the best in your endeavors!

Let's keep in touch! Become a subscriber to my email list. Don't worry, I won't fill your inbox with useless fluff. I will, however, send an occasional newsletter, industry news, or free giveaways. It's easy, simply go to cdwolfebooks.com to sign up. Quick and painless—I promise.

www.ingramcontent.com/pod-product-compliance
Lightning Source LLC
Chambersburg PA
CBHW071507220526
45472CB00003B/944